THE
CONSTITUTION
of
SILENCE

Contributions in Political Science
Series Editor: Bernard K. Johnpoll

Marvin Rintala

THE
CONSTITUTION
of
SILENCE

essays on
generational
themes

Contributions in Political Science, Number 25

GREENWOOD PRESS
Westport, Connecticut • London, England

Library of Congress Cataloging in Publication Data

Rintala, Marvin.
    The constitution of silence.

    (Contributions in political science ; no. 25
ISSN 0147-1066)
    Includes bibliographical references and index.
    1. Political sociology—Addresses, essays,
lectures. 2. Conflict of generations—Addresses,
essays, lectures. I. Title. II. Series.
JA76.R56   301.5'92   78-20018
ISBN 0-313-20723-2

Library of Congress Catalog Card Number: 78-20018
ISBN: 0-313-20723-2
ISSN: 0147-1066

First published in 1979

Greenwood Press, Inc.
51 Riverside Avenue, Westport, Connecticut 06880

Printed in the United States of America

10 9 8 7 6 5 4 3 2 1

In Memoriam
SIGMUND NEUMANN

Ja, der Geist spricht,
dass sie ruhen von ihrer Arbeit;
denn ihre Werke folgen ihnen nach.

Contents

Preface

These essays move in subject matter from the most general to the most specific. The first essay defines the meaning and relative significance of the concept of political generation. The second essay evaluates the impact of a particular historical event, World War I, upon a particular political generation, composed of those Europeans who were in their formative years—seventeen to twenty-five—during that event. The third essay explains serious conflict within a particular institution, the army, in a particular nation, Finland, by drawing upon generations theory. The focus shifts from the most general analytical discussion of generational consciousness in politics to the most detailed kind of application of generations theory in a case study. The second essay is therefore completely intelligible only in terms of the first essay, and the third essay only in terms of the first and second essays.

The arguments of the first essay are, one hopes, further buttressed by the utility, demonstrated in the second and third essays, of the concept of political generation for understanding particular political generations. The proof of the pudding for all social theory, including generations theory, is in the eating. The primary purpose of these essays is to use generations theory to understand political reality, not to evaluate that reality, let alone to reconstruct it. In this sense, in spite of external appearances, these essays owe more to Max Weber than to Karl Mannheim, although the former debt may be more general than the latter. For those readers whose taste in social science is less value free, these essays may nevertheless provide data useful for reconstructing political reality. Perhaps I may be permitted my own conclusion that generations theory essentially flows from one more iron cage encompassing the human condition.

Like most essays, these attempt to persuade. They are intended to encourage further research into political generations by students of politics at all levels of professional development. The audience to which these essays are primarily addressed is often, rightly or wrongly, at least partially persuaded by documentation. Notes have therefore been included, at the risk of intruding upon literary elegance, and a fourth, bibliographical, essay is included. These references are to a wide variety of sources, ranging from rigorous scholarship to autobiographical works to imaginative fiction. The intentional disparity of sources should offend no one who recognizes that politics is a many-splendored thing, and many ways of learning about it are therefore not only desirable but necessary.

As the notes reveal, many of my intellectual debts are to other authors who are or were not professional students of politics. These debts are at least revealed in the pages that follow, including the acknowledgments. Some of my debts, however, are to persons who were never guilty of authorship themselves—particularly elderly European gentlemen of diverse nations and classes who shared with me, often in convivial surroundings, their memories of the war they still call the Great War. They do not appear in the notes, but they taught me many things. I hope I have done them the justice of understanding them.

My greatest debt, nevertheless, is to a completely professional student of politics, and that debt is acknowledged—if not repaid—on the dedication page. Like all true teachers, Sigmund Neumann demonstrated that different generations *can* communicate with each other. Because he was so persuasive an advocate of the importance of generational consciousness in politics, the reader is burdened with the pages that follow. I am therefore in the happy position of not being solely responsible for any errors in these essays. They are just as much his as mine. This is equally true, of course, of any possible insights into political reality and into the human condition.

Acknowledgments

For permission to reprint quotations from published materials, grateful acknowledgment is made to:

Oxford University Press, for H. H. Gerth and C. Wright Mills, eds., *From Max Weber: Essays in Sociology* (New York: Oxford University Press, 1958);

Routledge and Kegan Paul Ltd. and Oxford University Press, for Karl Mannheim, *Essays on the Sociology of Knowledge*, ed. Paul Kecskemeti (London: Routledge and Kegan Paul Ltd., 1952);

Random House, for Marcel Proust, *Within a Budding Grove*, trans. C. K. Scott Moncrieff (New York: Vintage Books, 1970; copyright renewed 1951 by Random House, and Robert Penn Warren, *A Place to Come To* (New York: Random House, 1977; Copyright © 1977 by Robert Penn Warren);

Charles Scribner's Sons, for C. P. Snow, *Corridors of Power* (New York: Charles Scribner's Sons, 1964), and C. P. Snow, *The Search* (New York: The New American Library, 1960);

The Estate of the Late A. P. Herbert, for A. P. Herbert, *The Secret Battle*, 9th ed. (London: Methuen & Co. Ltd., 1949);

The Owen Estate, Chatto & Windus Ltd., and New Directions Publishing Corporation, for Wilfred Owen, *Collected Poems*, Copyright © Chatto & Windus, Ltd., 1946, 1963, reprinted by permission of New Directions;

Curtis Brown Ltd., on behalf of the Estate of Stuart Cloete, and Wm. Collins Sons & Co. Ltd., for Stuart Cloete, *How Young They Died* (London: Collins, 1969);

Maurice C. Greenbaum of Greenbaum, Wolff & Ernst, for Erich
    Maria Remarque, *The Road Back*, trans. A. W. Wheen (New
    York: Avon Books, 1959);
Simon and Schuster, for R. F. Delderfield, *To Serve Them All My
    Days* (New York: Simon and Schuster, 1972);
Little, Brown and Company, for Anthony Powell, *At Lady Molly's*
    (New York: Popular Library, 1976), and *The Iliad*, trans. from
    Homer by Alston Hurd Chase and William G. Perry, Jr. (No
    place: Little, Brown and Company, 1950);
Osbert Sitwell, Macmillan & Co. Ltd., and Little, Brown and Com-
    pany, for Osbert Sitwell, *Left Hand, Right Hand!* (London:
    Macmillan & Co. Ltd., 1952);
Oxford University Press, for Sir Ernest Barker, *Age and Youth:
    Memories of Three Universities and Father of the Man* (London,
    1953), by permission of Oxford University Press;
Horizon Press and Martin Secker & Warburg Limited, for quotations
    reprinted from *The Contrary Experience* by Herbert Read,
    copyright 1963, by permission of the publishers Horizon Press,
    New York, and Martin Secker & Warburg Limited, London;
Macdonald and Jane's Publishers Ltd. and A. M. Heath & Company
    Ltd., for Henry Williamson, *The Golden Virgin* (London:
    Macdonald, 1966);
Harcourt Brace Jovanovich, Inc., for a quotation, part of which is
    also used in the main title of this book, from "Little Gidding"
    in *Four Quartets*, copyright, 1943, by T. S. Eliot; renewed,
    1971, by Esme Valerie Eliot. Reprinted by permission of
    Harcourt Brace Jovanovich, Inc., which quotation is also from
    T. S. Eliot, *Collected Poems 1909-1962*, published by Faber
    and Faber Ltd.;
William Heinemann Ltd., for J. B. Priestley, *Margin Released: A
    Writer's Reminiscences and Reflections* (London: Heinemann,
    1962);
Farrar, Straus & Giroux, Inc., for *The Early Years of Alec Waugh*
    by Alec Waugh, Copyright © 1962 by Alec Waugh, published
    by Farrar, Straus and Company.

THE CONSTITUTION
of
SILENCE

Essay 1

Generations: Key to Politics?

C. P. Snow suggests that it is a short way to the grave for individual human beings, but the life of society can be made immortal.[1] Many of the groups to which human beings belong, of which they are conscious, and to which they feel a sense of allegiance and responsibility, such as their nation and their class, may indeed survive for centuries or perhaps even—as far as they will ever know— forever. There is, however, one group to which they belong that need not fear immortality: their generation. If, as is often assumed by students of politics, it is the sense of a common destiny that unites all French persons and all Germans, all members of the working class and of the middle class, surely no shared destiny is more fundamental than that of members of the same generation. These members have in common not necessarily language or income, but the agonies and triumphs of life itself.[2] Coevals who do not belong to the same class or nation may have more in common with each other than with members of the same class or nation who are not their coevals.[3]

If the ability to communicate helps to define membership in a group, one's generation exists both as an objective reality and—in human motivation, even more important—as a personal commitment. This ability to communicate is shared within a generation, but at the same time its members are cut off from other generations.[4] Some things one can share only with others of one's own age.[5] Even if, by some quirk of fate, one should wish to evade one's destiny as a member of a generation, one cannot. It has been argued that one can avoid any generational membership[6] and even that one can change one's generational membership.[7] Both are clearly impossible. Anyone who tries to escape from his or her generation is faced with cold, hard reality: "You belong to it, too. . . . You came along at the same time. You can't get away from it. You're a part of it whether you want to be or not."[8] An unwilling national can, if he or she is fortunate, migrate, and an unwilling member of a social class can often engage in social mobility, but there is nothing an unwilling member of a generation can do to alter his or her status. To live in his or her generation, or not to live at all, is the only choice left to a rebellious coeval. Every human being's generational membership is part of his or her inescapable fate.[9]

The fact that human beings consider themselvees to be divided into groups on the basis of generational differences is one of the great themes running through literature in all times and in all places. Generational conflict has been the basis of a good many literary careers. The frequency with which this theme recurs in literary works has perhaps been responsible for the emphasis that cultural historians have given to different literary, artistic, and musical generations. Sometimes, indeed, cultural historians have seen only the alternation of "romantic" and "classical" generations of artists. The alternation of generations may have explanatory value in biology, but probably not in the humanities or in the social sciences. Such an exaggerated emphasis forgets that there are fundamental continuities even in the creative arts,[10] and that no generation can be labeled—let alone dismissed—with one easy adjective. No generation is exactly the same as any other generation, for each has its own distinctive membership, experiences, problems, and destiny.

The uniqueness of each generation does not mean that generations cannot be subjected to comparative analysis. No groups studied by the comparative method are, after all, entirely similar; if they were, the comparative method would be far less interesting and valuable than it is. The comparative method involves the search for dissimilarities as well as similarities. It would be reasonable to expect that both sociologists and political scientists might find generations intriguing as a concept and as a tool of scientific analysis. Sociologists have, in fact, devoted substantial attention to generational differences, and most of the important statements of generational theory have been the work of sociologists.

For the most part, however, political scientists have given little thought to the possibility that a generational approach might help to understand some otherwise inexplicable aspects of politics. In particular, it is surprising that students of comparative politics, who have made such extensive use of nation and class as tools of analysis, have virtually ignored generational differences. For all practical purposes, study of generational differences in politics has been confined to totalitarian political systems and totalitarian movements within democratic political systems, with a few forays into explaining individual political leaders in terms of their generational membership. If generations theory has any validity, it should be applied to a wide variety of questions dealing with the motivation of leaders and followers in all political movements and systems, not merely those that are totalitarian.

Generational consciousness is undoubtedly less significant as a source of political motivation than either national or class consciousness. National consciousness finds its organizational expression in national states, and class consciousness finds its organizational expression in class-based parties. There is no analogous organizational structure created by generational consciousness,[11] other than loosely knit groups such as "Young Turks," "Young Germany,"[12] "Young England,"[13] "Young Wales,"[14] or "Young Conservatives." There are many powerful politicians recognized as primarily national or class leaders, but there are relatively few such politicians recognized as primarily generational leaders. Some political leaders nevertheless write autobiographies entitled My Generation of Politics and Politicians, or simply My Generation.[15] Indeed, perhaps the most impressive evidence for the existence of generational consciousness in politics is the frequency with which it is articulated in the autobiographical writings of political leaders. These writings suggest that generational consciousness is an important, if not predominant, motivation for political thought and action, and that the study of generational differences in politics should therefore be widespread among political scientists. Generations theory is not the key to understanding politics, but it is certainly a key.

The relative lack of interest in generational consciousness among political scientists is unfortunate, especially since group consciousness is universally recognized as one of the fundamental elements of political motivation. Individual human beings in every political

system seek the security provided by membership in groups. Dostoevsky's Grand Inquisitor may have overstated his case when he
referred to the yearning of human beings for "one unanimous and
harmonious ant heap,"[16] but he had a point. Group consciousness
is created by certain perceived basic similarities among individual
human beings and this consciousness in turn creates more homo-
geneity within the group, a conformity that often leads to common
action. Individuals think of themselves as members of a group,
and therefore frequently act as members of that group. Since the
perceived interests of different groups are not always compatible,
there is social conflict. Since all individuals have allegiances to
more than one group, there is conflict within the individual as well,
for he or she must decide which group, if any, is most important in
given circumstances. In European politics, for instance, there has
often been conflict between national consciousness and class consciousness, which has generally been resolved in favor of the former,
most dramatically in 1914.

The skepticism of political scientists towards a generations approach is, quite probably, mainly due to uncertainty among most
political scientists about the precise meaning of the concept of
political generation. It would serve no useful purpose to advocate
use by political scientists of this concept—as I do—without having
a clear-cut understanding of its meaning. Confusion about its
meaning appears to be widespread among those sympathetic to a
generational approach as well as those who are critical of such an
approach. A generational approach all too frequently has been
embraced as well as rejected out of ignorance. Perhaps the two
most common erroneous assumptions about generations theory are
the separate but related assumptions that a political generation is
the same as a biological generation,[17] and that there are always two
generations in politics at any one time.

Whatever else it may be, a political generation is not the same as
a biological generation.[18] Political generations do not suddenly
"change" every thirty or thirty-five years. The process of social,
including political, change is continuous, and it cannot wait until
political power, economic wealth, or social prestige is handed on
from father to son. Generations theory has very little in common
with psychological theories about fathers and sons, whether those
theories are expressed in fiction or in social scientific literature. It is

certainly an extreme overstatement, for instance, to argue: "The history, political style, and future development of a political community reflect the quality of the relationship between fathers and sons."[19] There is undoubtedly much personal conflict between fathers and sons, but most of this conflict has no direct political significance. The history of politics is not the history of conflict, or even of consensus, between fathers and sons, although such conflict may take place, as it did between James and John Stuart Mill, with important political consequences.[20] Children may confuse the authority of the ruler with the authority of the father,[21] but adults active in political life are hardly likely to remain so confused.

Perhaps the most important exceptions to this statement are, in fact, those dynastic sons who are likely to inherit political power directly and automatically from their fathers. For such atypical sons, fathers are in fact also rulers, and these equally atypical fathers are confronted by subjects who are also their own sons, and who possess just as much genetic legitimacy as their fathers. This situation has often provided the basis for political conflict. Long before there were opposition parties in the modern sense, there were court factions supporting aspiring sons as well as ruling fathers. Crown princes and other potential heirs of traditional authority have been notoriously unfaithful to their fathers during the lifetimes of the latter.[22] It may well be that the novelist's perception was correct:

"Take it as a rule," this sardonic old Eaves would say, "the fathers and elder sons of all great families hate each other. The Crown Prince is always in opposition to the crown or hankering after it. . . . And it stands to reason that every great man, having experienced this feeling towards his father, must be aware that his son entertains it towards himself; and so they can't but be suspicious and hostile."[23]

It also may well be, however, that in such circumstances a son may have hated his father because he loved power, rather than loved power because he hated his father. With the passing of Weber's traditional type of authority,[24] such father-son conflicts have become less important in political reality, if not in Freudian flights of fancy.

It should be noted that generations theory does not preclude political conflict between adult sons and their fathers caused by essentially divergent experiences in their respective formative years,[25] but the causes here would be broadly social rather than narrowly psychological. Generations theory, furthermore, does not preclude political cooperation between adult sons and their fathers caused by essentially similar experiences in their respective formative years. Not all intergenerational relationships in politics are based on conflict—some are based on cooperation, although, assuming a minimal rate of social change, conflict is likely to overshadow cooperation.

If a political generation is not the same as a biological generation, what is it? It could most conveniently be defined as a group of human beings who have undergone the same basic historical experiences during their formative years. Given this definition, it is important to limit both the time span and the spatial span within which all who experience their formative years can be said to be molded into one distinct political generation. Without such limits, it is impossible to classify individual human beings as members of one political generation with any precision. Such classification cannot be done scientifically on an ad hoc basis. If the latter basis is used, it may be properly suspected that generational differences are being used as a *deus ex machina*, as a court of last resort in much the same way that differences in national character are appealed to when there seems to be no other explanation of some political phenomenon.

The concept of political generation, nevertheless, is intimately related to the process of social change. Any arbitrary choice of the time span within which one distinct political generation is formed is likely to do injustice to social reality. How long it takes to form one political generation depends upon the relative rapidity of social change. When social change is very slow, it is difficult to distinguish between generations.[26] Indeed, if social stagnation is approached, it is possible that there might be only one political generation in existence at a given time. In this case, generational explanations would not be helpful in understanding the causes for whatever political conflicts existed, although such explanations might be very helpful in understanding the causes for such political stability as existed.

When social change is very rapid, generational differences are magnified.[27] The distinctiveness of each generation is a function of the rate of social change.[28] This rate varies widely with time and space.[29] This means the time span needed to form a distinct generation varies widely over time and space. Alexis de Tocqueville perceived this clearly:

Among aristocratic nations, as families remain for centuries in the same condition, often on the same spot, all generations become, as it were, contemporaneous. . . . Among democratic nations new families are constantly springing up, others are constantly falling away, and all that remain change their condition; the woof of time is in every instant broken and the track of generations effaced.[30]

The helpfulness of de Tocqueville's insight remains, even though today one would replace "aristocratic" with "premodern," and "democratic" with "modern." Perhaps unfortunately, de Tocqueville's equation of modernity with democracy has not proved justified.

Such considerations as de Tocqueville's undoubtedly led Karl Mannheim to conclude: "Whether a new *generation style* emerges every year, every thirty, every hundred years, or whether it emerges rhythmically at all, depends entirely on the trigger action of the social and cultural processes."[31] This is merely one aspect, of course, of the general problem of applying ideal types to concrete situations. Since all concepts of comparative analysis must be defined in time and space, generations theory is not alone in facing this problem of providing sufficient analytical precision without oversimplifying social reality. This problem *is* especially significant for generations theory, however, since membership in one political generation involves a common location in time and space.[32] Some answer therefore must be provided to the question: what is the time span needed to form a political generation?

The answers given to this question have varied widely.[33] At least some of this variation can be explained by overgeneralization from a limited number of cases or even from one case. The most reasonable estimate for the time span required to form a political generation in twentieth-century Western society is probably ten to fifteen years. Given the fact that the rate of social change in twentieth-century Western society is very rapid and perhaps even cataclysmic,[34] this period is probably shorter than in most other times and places. Given the fact that this rate seems to be increasing,[35] the time span needed to form one political generation is likely to shorten further during the foreseeable future.

Although the spatial span of a political generation is equally difficult to limit with precision, it is clear that many coevals are not members of the same political generation. Those whose formative experiences are fundamentally different cannot be members of the same political generation, even though they may coexist in time.[36] There was, for instance, no real community of experience between young people in China and Germany in 1800.[37] It could, however, be argued that there is considerable community of experience between young people in East Germany and Communist China today, since their formative years are taking place in totalitarian political systems. Such phenomena as the spread of nationalism and of industrialization and urbanization suggest that the spatial barriers "between" generations may be breaking down, at the same time that more rapid social change is increasing the importance of the temporal barriers "between" generations. The effect of the latter development is to make communication between different political generations more difficult, while the effect of the former development, by making political generations larger in spatial terms, is to increase the worldwide significance of this decline in ability to communicate. The implications of these long-range developments for meaningful communication within and among political systems are not entirely encouraging. The political generations formed in Europe by the Franco-Prussian War, World War I, and World War II were progressively larger, but the increase in the size of the generational political community did not lead to greater political stability for Europe.

Given the life expectancy predominant in modern Western societies, the mistaken equation of political and biological generations encourages the second major misconception about generations theory, that there are two and only two political generations existing at any one time. We saw earlier that there might be only one political generation at a given time. With the relatively rapid rate of social change characteristic of twentieth-century Western societies—and, increasingly, non-Western societies as well—there are likely to be more than two generations in politics at any one time.[38] These several generations will coexist in time and space, but they are likely to experience serious difficulties in communicating with each other,[39] and it is extremely uncertain whether peaceful coexistence among them is possible. The assumption common in many political systems—democratic as well as totalitarian—that the only generational participants in the political process at a given time are a "young" generation and an "old" generation is as badly oversimplified as Karl Marx's assumption that there are only two social classes in modern industrial society.

The assumption that there are at any moment in time two political generations, and that these two generations are always in conflict, is frequently linked with the equally mistaken corollary that the "young" generation is "liberal," and the "old" generation is "conservative."[40] That this corollary is also erroneous is evident from the fact that there have been many cases of some younger generation being more conservative than some older generation.[41] Aging does not inevitably produce conservatism any more than youth inevitably produces liberalism. Octogenarians are not necessarily reactionaries, and young men and women are not necessarily revolutionaries.

The political implications, if any, of the process of biological aging are still unclear.[42] What is clear is that generations theory is at least potentially contradictory to theories emphasizing the impact of aging on political thought and action. Generations theory assumes that political commitments of individual adult human beings do not undergo substantial change over time.[43] Generations theory therefore contradicts the prevalent assumption[44] in political science that political socialization is a lifelong process. For generations theory: "We must ask not how old the elector is but when it was that he was young."[45] Both generational and aging theories may have their usefulness in explaining political reality, but they cannot explain the same segment of political reality. They are therefore in a very real sense competitive theories,[46] and it is highly unlikely that any individual student of politics could believe that they have equal explanatory value. For individual human beings, in political science as in politics, it is often a matter of either-or.[47] There are clearly established differences among generations of scholars, including political scientists,[48] and it is quite likely that these differences result from the decisive impact of different experiences in the formative years of scholars.[49] These differences may well be desirable in view of the possibility that "in political science, a major impulse to development is the . . . conflict of generations."[50] Perhaps, furthermore, generations theory itself explains why some scholars have accepted the validity of this theory and others have not?[51]

Scholarship is not the only field of human activity where attitudes once taken do not undergo substantial change during the lifetime of the holders of these attitudes. Politics is no different in this respect. Once a set of political beliefs has been embraced, it is unlikely that an individual human being will abandon his or her beliefs. Rather than altering their previous outlook on the basis of new facts, human beings either reject or embrace these facts, depending on whether these facts fit comfortably into their previous outlook. Political educability ends after the formative years.[52] Openness to new ideas[53] and new experiences[54] is then minimal. Human beings become unpersuadable,[55] and, as a writer hostile to a generational approach concedes, new political events are perceived in terms of preexisting outlooks.[56] In short, the personality has been formed.[57] Each person's "character has set like plaster, and will never soften again."[58] Just as it is difficult to learn a new language without an accent after the formative years,[59] it is difficult to learn a new political language. The "memory sponge is getting soggy."[60] As an eminently realistic observer put it, even a man of thirty will have much to learn in the course of his lifetime, but this will only supplement and fill in the framework provided him by the personal philosophy he has already adopted.[61] All the creative ideas are already there.[62] This is true of other creative arts, not merely scholarship, besides politics.[63] It is even true of such noncreative artisans as civil servants.[64]

In this sense, a "liberal" generation will remain "liberal" throughout the adult lifetime of its members. Whether this same political attitude will appear liberal under radically changed circumstances is, of course, uncertain. Much of the confusion in the political vocabulary of any political system is due to the different meanings given to the same term by members of different political generations. Herbert Hoover's liberalism, for instance, always remained very real to him even though younger generations in American politics considered liberalism to have a social rather than an individual connotation. More generally, in the United States an individual who became a Wilsonian liberal in his formative years might have considered himself entirely consistent in voting for Republican candidates after the Democratic Party was transformed in 1933 under Franklin Roosevelt. A committed Zionist might well change parties, which are simply means to an end.[65] A supporter of the Congress Party at the achievement of Indian independence might in later decades feel that his or her continuing personal beliefs were best articulated by some other—or by no—party. It may well be true that: "It was the Parties which had changed—not Winston."[66] These considerations suggest that in further research on generational differences in politics care should be taken not to concentrate exclusively on any single element of political action, such as party identification or, what is in an American context perilously close to the same thing, voting behavior. Since the same fundamental personal attitudes might cause a voter to shift party allegiance in a changing party constellation, consistency—or inconsistency—in voting behavior is not a crucial test of the persistence of personal attitudes over time. This, of course, is a danger signal that research into voting behavior has not always heeded.

Whether a political leader or follower ought to change his or her vocabulary to suit the needs—or whims—of a changed situation is outside the scope of this book. It is perhaps worth noting, however, that in explaining the tenacity of "outmoded" policies, a generational approach removes these policies from the realm of free choice by political leaders and followers and therefore from the realm of possible moral judgments by political scientists. In this respect, a generational approach has the same kinds of weaknesses and strengths as any other determinist approach,[67] although it should therefore have a special appeal to political scientists who want to remain value free. If it is difficult to label a generation with descriptive terms, it is much more difficult—and much less justifiable—to label one generation "good" and another generation "bad." Students of political generations, just as students of parties and political systems, should not play favorites.

If political attitudes, once formed, are not likely to change, it is important to know precisely at what period of life these attitudes are formed. The greatest single contribution of generations theory is that it provides an intelligible, meaningful, and internally consistent answer to this question. Significantly, no serious advocate of a generational approach has argued that political attitudes are formed during childhood.[68] Generations theory takes sharp issue with the assumption that the "truly formative years of the maturing member of a political system" are "the years between the ages of three and thirteen."[69] There seems little reason to assume that the child is father to the political man. It remains to be seen whether it can be demonstrated that the political attitudes, let alone the forms of political action, of a forty-year-old adult human being are those he or she accepted as a child of four years. Even the existing body of generalizations linking childhood experience to adult behavior is rudimentary.[70] If this is true of generalizations, it is doubly true of evidence.[71] Furthermore, anyone who has the slightest desire to believe in the possibility of rational political life should view the alternative possibility that the child is indeed father to the man with the most profound fear and trembling.

Rather than assuming that childhood years are decisive in the process of political socialization, it seems more sensible to assume that nothing of real political significance happens during those years. Even at the end of childhood, the human personality is virtually a *tabula rasa*.[72] This is certainly more credible than the assumption that personality development "is at its peak" during childhood,[73] or that "childhood rivals and probably surpasses the later years in its importance for the political growth of the individual."[74]

It is not childhood, but late adolescence and early adulthood—that age of human beings called youth—that according to generations theory, are the formative years during which a distinctive personal world view, which remains unchanged in its fundamentals through old age, is created. The crucial years in the formation of political attitudes are seen, at least in modern Western societies, as those from approximately seventeen to twenty-five. For a minority the formative years may begin slightly earlier or later, and for a minority the formative years may end slightly earlier or later, but these exceptions are seen as relatively insignificant. If these years are truly formative, of course, neither the years before nor the years after them are decisive in the formation of political attitudes.

The leading generations theorist explained the choice of seventeen as the beginning of the formative years:

The possibility of really questioning and reflecting on things only emerges at the point where personal experimentation with life begins—round about the age of 17, sometimes a little earlier and sometimes a little later. It is only then that life's problems begin to be located in a "present" and are experienced as such. That level of data and attitudes which social change has rendered problematical, and which therefore requires reflection, has now been reached; for the first time, one lives "in the present."[75]

The validity of Mannheim's hypothesis is supported by a wide variety of evidence. At the beginning of the formative years it seems to the emerging human personality that he or she is "beginning to awake to life,"[76] and that his or her life really begins.[77] At this age even unpleasant experiences can be seen as valuable, because they are the occasions for the beginning of one's mental life.[78] With the beginning of an independent mental existence one is finally really born.[79] These mental birth pangs can be quite painful,[80] but also the cause for considerable self-pride.[81] The concept "I," previously meaningless, assumes content and meaning.[82] If the self *has* existed in childhood it has remained "wholly transcendental and out of sight."[83] In later trying to remember childhood, "I don't see myself."[84]

The experience of a young university student in a Finnish novel is perhaps typical of all those in their formative years all over the world: "During the previous winter he had experienced a miracle, in that he realized that he existed. He had begun to grasp that there existed such a person as Ilmari Salpakari. Some kind of breakthrough had taken place, and he really couldn't say how. He had just gradually noticed that many matters appeared differently from before."[85] At the beginning of the formative years, those things that have been clear become confused, and those things—especially concerning the future—that have been confused become clear.[86] The human personality that is coming into being not only recognizes its existence, but understands that it is in a process of constant development.[87] It must listen more to its own inner voices.[88] It no longer believes everything it sees and hears.[89] As an articulate refugee

from the Soviet Union put it: "After children begin to live inde-
pendently, around the age of 17 or so, they see things differently. It
is one thing for their parents to support them, and another thing for
a person to earn for himself. No, after a person is 23 or 25, none of
the earlier illusions of 10 or 15 remain."[90]

If political and other forms of social cynicism are products of the
formative years, so is faith in one's own judgment. During the
formative years the youth begins to form his or her own taste[91]
and to adopt causes.[92] He or she acquires new premises not only for
self-identity but for "the whole of this world."[93] He or she recognizes
that there is a larger world outside his or her immediate family and
peers.[94] For the first time he or she acquires a clear conception of
the fact that his or her immediate circle is not alone in the world,
and that there exist other lives, the lives of people who have nothing
in common with his or her immediate circle and who do not have
the slightest idea that this circle exists: "Without a doubt I had
known all this before; but not in the way I became aware of it now;
I had not been conscious of it, had not felt it."[95]

That a perception of the self is taking place at the same time as a
perception of society is no accident. An important part of the discovery of self-identity is the definition of who one is in society.[96]
When he or she discovers whom he or she is in social terms, the
youth becomes politically conscious. Political consciousness
therefore begins during the formative years of youth, not during
childhood.[97] The result is that the youth takes his or her first independent social actions.[98] He or she starts in a very real sense to lead
a life of his or her own.[99] He or she forms, for the first and perhaps
last time, lifelong personal friendships—and enmities.[100] One need
not accept Carl Schmitt's view of politics as the opposition of friend
and foe[101] to recognize the political significance of friendships and
enmities originating in the formative years. The most important
aspect of this independent life, of course, is the choice of a vocation: "You discovered yourself, deciding what kinds of things you
wanted to do in life and with what kinds of person you wanted to
do them."[102] It is possible that this discovery very clearly means
that politics is not one's vocation.[103] It is even possible to discover
that one has politics as a vocation.[104] It was therefore no accident
that the greatest of all Max Weber's sermons was addressed ʰo

university students who were wondering whether politics was their vocation, and that he ended by asking whether each listener was "sure that he shall not crumble when the world from his point of view is too stupid or too base for what he wants to offer. Only he who in the face of all this can say 'In spite of all!' has the calling for politics."[105]

Weber was clearly appealing for a lifetime commitment to a cause as the precondition for a political career. That his appeal was not unrealistic appears equally clear. The persistence of political attitudes, once adopted during the formative years, is notable. This is true of followers[106] as well as of leaders.[107] Most leaders and most followers could state accurately that "I haven't altered much as I've got older."[108] It is not individual human beings who change, but rather the social context in which they exist. The great dreams that political leaders attempt to realize are the dreams of their political youth.[109] To use Max Weber's terminology, the cause a particular leader serves comes from his or her formative years. As the aged Adenauer revealed, "when I was twenty-five years old I already had this idea that the European countries should go together more closely."[110] In eulogizing President J. K. Paasikivi, the Speaker of the Finnish Parliament accurately summarized Paasikivi's sixty years of Finnish politics as a vocation:

Believing as a young man that by a conciliatory attitude towards the Czarist regime the Finnish people could have a chance to live its own life in peace, beneath the shadow of the great neighbor, he had suffered disappointment. After pondering on this question for decades, he had found that a similar attitude was still the only solution. . . . After the [Second World] war he was in a position [as President] to decisively influence the pages of Finnish history when the great concept of his youth proved to be right—the possibility of relaxing the state of tension on the eastern border without jeopardizing the country's independence or her inherited social values.[111]

Rather than leading to a renunciation of youthful dreams, the passage of years solidifies them and surrounds them with a romantic glow. Hugh Dalton, whose performance as Chancellor of the Exchequer was hardly that of a romantic, remembered his formative years:

I date my political awakening from an evening at Cambridge, now more than twenty years ago, when I helped to form a bodyguard for Keir Hardie and protect him from physical violence at the hands of some of my fellow undergraduates. Most of the fighters on both sides in that gay little battle are dead now, having passed through very different battles to the Great Peace. That evening I sat at Keir Hardie's feet, both literally and spiritually. He made me a Socialist and lighted in my heart a flame of hope which is burning still, though the war came near to putting it out.[112]

Even a more realistic recollection of his or her formative years by a political leader may demonstrate the persistence of political attitudes. In 1831 Chief Justice Bushe remarked:

I have read over a pamphlet which I wrote in 1791 when in my twenty-fifth year, and though my better, at least older, judgment and taste condemn some instances of hasty and erroneous opinions rashly hazarded, much superficial and inaccurate reasoning,—yet at the end of forty years, I abide by most of the principles that I then maintained.[113]

Léon Blum summed up his own political career,[114] as well as the case for a generational approach to the study of politics, when he observed: "A man remains essentially what his youth has made him."[115] Blum's observation may have been an expression of a commonplace truth, but it was an expression of a truth that political science can ignore only at its own risk. For even relatively sophisticated political animals, "my encounter with history" becomes "my generation's encounter with history."[116] How this transformation takes place is an important item on the agenda of political science.

NOTES

1. *The New Men* (New York: Charles Scribner's Sons, 1954), p. 301.

2. Harold Macmillan, *Winds of Change 1914-1939* (New York: Harper & Row, 1966), pp. 80-81; José Ortega y Gasset, *Man and Crisis*, trans. Mildred Adams (New York: W. W. Norton & Company, 1958), p. 44; José Ortega y Gassett, *Man and People*, trans. Willard R. Trask (New York: W. W. Norton & Sons, 1963), pp. 157-58.

3. Ralph Waldo Emerson, *Representative Men: Seven Lectures* (Boston: Houghton Mifflin Company, 1876), p. 26; Jussi Talvi, *Isänmaa: Romaani* (Helsinki: Kustannusosakeyhtiö Otava, 1960), p. 16; A. J. P. Taylor, *The*

Course of German History: A Survey of the Development of Germany since 1815 (New York: Coward-McCann, 1946), p. 130.

4. Emerson, *Representative Men*, p. 26; C. P. Snow, *The Light and the Dark* (New York: Charles Scribner's Sons, 1964), pp. 50, 227, 253, 281; Leo Tolstoy, *Childhood, Boyhood and Youth*, trans. Michael Scammell (New York: McGraw-Hill Book Company, 1965), p. 315.

5. Karl Mannheim, "The Problem of Generations," in his *Essays on the Sociology of Knowledge*, ed. Paul Kecskemeti (London: Routledge and Kegan Paul Ltd., 1952), p. 283; C. P. Snow, *The Sleep of Reason* (New York: Charles Scribner's Sons, 1968), p. 116.

6. T. S. Eliot, *The Complete Poems and Plays 1909-1950* (New York: Harcourt, Brace & World, 1971), p. 227; Matti Kurjensaari, *Suomalainen päiväkirja: 20 vuotta sitten: Uudet päätelmät* (Helsinki: Kustannusosakeyhtiö Tammi, 1976), p. 11.

7. Myron Weiner and Samuel P. Huntington, Preface, and William Quandt, "Generational Change in the Arab World," in *Political Generations and Political Development*, ed. Richard J. Samuels (Lexington, Mass.: D. C. Heath and Company, 1977), pp. vii, 84.

8. Thomas Wolfe, *You Can't Go Home Again* (New York: Grosset & Dunlap, no date), p. 715. For Wolfe's perception of his own generation, see C. Hugh Holman and Sue Fields Ross, eds., *The Letters of Thomas Wolfe to His Mother* (Chapel Hill: The University of North Carolina Press, 1968), p. 160.

9. Martin Heidegger, quoted by Mannheim, "The Problem of Generations," p. 282; José Ortega y Gasset, quoted by Julián Marías, *Reason and Life: The Introduction to Philosophy*, trans. Kenneth S. Reid and Edward Sarmiento (New Haven: Yale University Press, 1956), p. 361; J. B. Priestley, *Margin Released: A Writer's Reminiscences and Reflections* (London: Heinemann, 1962), p. 31; Richard Aldington, *Death of a Hero* (London: Chatto & Windus, 1929), p. 334; Sholto Douglas, *Years of Combat* (London: Collins, 1963), p. 339; Margaret Mead, *Blackberry Winter: My Earlier Years* (New York: William Morrow & Company, 1972), p. 5.

10. Wilfred Dunwell, *Music and the European Mind* (New York: Thomas Yoseloff, 1962), p. 149.

11. There are occasional exceptions to this statement, as suggested by Kalle Lehmus, *Tuntematon Mannerheim: Katkelmia sodan ja politiikan poluilta* (Helsinki: Weilin & Göös, 1967), pp. 196-97.

12. Helen M. Mustard, ed. *Heinrich Heine: Selected Works* (New York: Vintage Books, 1973), p. xvii.

13. Walter Sichel, Introduction, in Benjamin Disraeli, *Sybil or the Two Nations* (London: Oxford University Press, 1975), p. vi.

14. Jack Jones, *The Man David: An Imaginative Presentation, Based on Fact, of the Life of David Lloyd George from 1880 to 1914* (London: Hamish Hamilton, 1944), p. 42.

15. W. T. R. Preston, *My Generation of Politics and Politicians* (Toronto: D. A. Rose Publishing Company, 1927); Will Paynter, *My Generation* (London: George Allen & Unwin Ltd., 1972).

16. Fyodor Dostoevsky, *The Brothers Karamazov*, trans. Constance Garnett (New York: Random House, 1950), p. 306.

17. This error is made even in conceptually sophisticated studies, as when it is argued that "a generation is still a generation in politics." Karl Deutsch et al., *Political Community and the North Atlantic Area: International Organization in the Light of Historical Experiences* (Princeton: Princeton University Press, 1957), p. 12; see also Philip W. Buck, *Amateurs and Professionals in British Politics 1918-59* (Chicago: The University of Chicago Press, 1963), p. 6. A generation may still be a generation in biology, but this says nothing about a political generation.

18. Marías, *Reason and Life*, pp. 359-62; Lewis S. Feuer, *The Conflict of Generations: The Character and Significance of Student Movements* (New York: Basic Books, 1969), p. 25.

19. Robert E. Lane, "Fathers and Sons: Foundations of Political Belief," *American Sociological Review* 24 (August 1959): 511.

20. The latter described his own agonizing reappraisal during his early twenties in the *Autobiography of John Stuart Mill* (New York: Columbia University Press, 1924), p. 126. For a classic statement of a father-son conflict, see Norbert Wiener, *Ex-Prodigy: My Childhood and Youth* (Cambridge: The M.I.T. Press, 1972), pp. 68-81.

21. There is evidence to suggest that not even children are so childish. Robert D. Hess and Judith V. Torney, *The Development of Political Attitudes in Children* (Garden City, N.Y.: Doubleday & Company, 1968), p. 115.

22. Some interesting examples are: Lavender Cassels, *Clash of Generations: A Habsburg Family Drama in the Nineteenth Century* (Newton Abbot: Victorian [and Modern History] Book Club, 1974), p. 124; Winston S. Churchill, *My Early Life: A Roving Commission* (New York: Charles Scribner's Sons, 1963), pp. 31, 33, 36, 38-40, 46, 48, 62; Stig Jägerskiöld, *Ruori Mannerheim*, trans. Sirkka Rapola (Helsinki: Kustannusosakeyhtiö Otava, 1964), pp. 56-58, 70, 80, 87, 90, 177, 186, 188, 194-95, 246, 285-86, 296, 299, 303, 305, 309, 311-12, 371; Stig Jägerskiöld, *Gustaf Mannerheim 1906-1917*, trans. Sirkka Rapola (Helsinki: Kustannusosakeyhtiö Otava, 1965), p. 202; *A King's Story: The Memoirs of the Duke of Windsor* (New York: G. P. Putnam's Sons, 1951), pp. 132, 190; J. H. Plumb, *The First Four Georges* (London: B. T. Batsford Ltd., 1956), pp. 42, 51-52, 55, 59, 83;

Roger Fulford, *George the Fourth* (New York: Capricorn Books, 1963), pp. 22, 27; Basil Herbert, *King Gustave of Sweden* (London: Stanley Paul & Co., Ltd., 1938), pp. 76-78; Joyce Cary, *Prisoner of Grace* (New York: Harper & Brothers, 1952), pp. 139, 192.

23. William Makepeace Thackeray, *Vanity Fair: A Novel Without a Hero* (New York: The New American Library, 1962), p. 556.

24. Max Weber, *The Theory of Social and Economic Organization*, ed. Talcott Parsons and trans. A. M. Henderson and Talcott Parsons (New York: The Free Press of Glencoe, 1964), pp. 341-58.

25. Kaspar D. Naegele, "Youth and Society: Some Observations," *Daedalus*, Winter 1962, p. 49.

26. Walter Bagehot, *Physics and Politics* (Boston: Beacon Press, 1956), pp. 46-47. The ease with which such a slow rate of social change can accelerate is clear from Herbert du Parcq, *Life of David Lloyd George*, vol. III (London: Caxton Publishing Co., Ltd., 1913), p. 521.

27. Kenneth Keniston, "Social Change and Youth in America," *Daedalus*, Winter 1962, p. 153; Robert Jay Lifton, "Youth and History: Individual Change in Postwar Japan," *Daedalus*, Winter 1962, p. 194; Feuer, *The Conflict of Generations*, p. 26.

28. Montgomery of Alamein, *The Path to Leadership* (London: Collins, 1961), p. 159. Comte had it backwards: he thought the rate of social change was a function of the distance between generations. Marías, *Reason and Life*, p. 179. Unfortunately Marías also had it backwards, as evident from Julián Marías, *Generations: A Historical Method*, trans. Harold C. Raley (University, Ala.: The University of Alabama Press, 1970), p. 168.

29. Alistair Cooke, *A Generation on Trial: U.S.A. v. Alger Hiss* (New York: Alfred A. Knopf, 1950), p. 41.

30. *Democracy in America*, vol. II (New York: Vintage Books, 1958), pp. 104-5.

31. Mannheim, "The Problem of Generations," p. 310; see also Sidney Verba, in Samuels, ed., *Political Generations and Political Development*, p. 21. The "rhythmic choruses of generations" are heard too clearly by Harold C. Raley, *José Ortega y Gasset: Philosopher of European Unity* (University, Ala.: The University of Alabama Press, 1971), p. 27.

32. Ortega y Gasset, *Man and Crisis*, p. 44.

33. Some examples are: W. L. Burn, *The Age of Equipoise: A Study of the Mid-Victorian Generation* (New York: W. W. Norton & Company, 1965), p. 15; Churchill, *My Early Life*, p. 59; Reuel Denney, "American Youth Today: A Bigger Cast, A Wider Screen," *Daedalus*, Winter 1962, p. 125; Tyyni Tuulio, "Pappilan kasvatti," in *Ilon ja aatteen vuodet*, ed. Toini Havu (Hämeenlinna: Arvi A. Karisto Osakeyhtiö, 1965), p. 42; Samuel P. Huntington, in Samuels, ed., *Political Generations and Political*

Development, p. 25; Mervyn Jones, *Holding On* (London: Quartet Books, 1973), p. 141; Christer Kihlman, "Sukupolvien vastakohtaisuus," in *60-luvun perspektiivi*, ed. Lars Dufholm, Ralf Friberg, and N-B. Stormbom, and trans. Jorma Aaltonen (Jyväskylä: K. J. Gummerus Osakeyhtiö, 1961), p. 236; Arthur Koestler, *The Yogi and the Commissar and Other Essays* (New York: Collier Books, 1961), p. 53; Marías, *Generations*, pp. 155, 157, 185-86; Marías, *Reason and Life*, p. 361; Raley, *José Ortega y Gasset*, p. 52; Erich Maria Remarque, *All Quiet on the Western Front* (New York: Fawcett World Library, 1964), p. 25; Erich Maria Remarque, *Three Comrades*, trans. A. W. Wheen (New York: Popular Library, 1964), pp. 103-4; Maurice Sachs, *Witches' Sabbath*, trans. Richard Howard (New York: Ballantine Books, 1966), p. 159; Ortega y Gasset, *Man and Crisis*, pp. 60, 65; Alfred C. Stepan, "The Concept of Generations in Military Institutions: Brazil and Peru Compared," in Samuels, ed., *Political Generations and Political Development*, p. 57; Erich Zimmermann and Hans-Adolf Jacobsen, eds., *Germans against Hitler: July 20, 1944* (Bonn: Berto-Verlag, 1960), p. 220.

34. Heinrich Böll, quoted by Michael Hamburger, "The Cult of Success: on 'the Battle of a Book,'" *Encounter* 22 (April 1964):120; Churchill, *My Early Life*, pp. 67, 90-91, 370; Raymond B. Fosdick, *Chronicle of a Generation: An Autobiography* (New York: Harper & Brothers, 1958), pp. 2, 289; Keniston, "Social Change and Youth in America," p. 152; Sigmund Neumann, *Permanent Revolution: Totalitarianism in the Age of International Civil War*, 2nd ed. (New York: Frederick A. Praeger, 1965), p. 234; Walter Z. Laqueur, *Young Germany: A History of the German Youth Movement* (New York: Basic Books, 1962), p. 48; Sir John Slessor, *These Remain: A Personal Anthology* (London: Michael Joseph, 1969), p. 163; Konstantin Paustovsky, *The Story of a Life*, trans. Joseph Barnes (New York: Pantheon Books, 1964), pp. 258-59.

35. Keniston, "Social Change and Youth in America," p. 150; Paynter, *My Generation*, p. 7.

36. Marías, *Generations*, p. 167; Ortega y Gasset, *Man and Crisis*, p. 43; Anselm L. Strauss, *Mirrors and Masks: The Search for Identity* (Glencoe, Ill.: The Free Press, 1959), p. 138.

37. Mannheim, "The Problem of Generations," p. 298.

38. Marías, *Reason and Life*, pp. 19-20, 359.

39. Wilhelm Dilthey, *Pattern and Meaning in History: Thoughts on History and Society* (New York: Harper & Brothers, 1961), p. 153; Benjamin Disraeli, *Coningsby or, The New Generation* (New York: Capricorn Books, 1961), p. 391; Michael Rywkin, "Generations in Conflict: The Literary Arena," *Problems of Communism* 13 (July-August 1964): 7; Mika

Waltari, *Isästä poikaan:romaani kolmen sukupolven Helsingistä* (Porvoo: Werner Söderström Osakeyhtiö, 1960), p. 179.

40. The latter assumption is made by even relatively cautious observers: Harvey C. Lehman, *Age and Achievement* (Princeton: Princeton University Press, 1953), p. 330; Maurice Duverger, *Political Parties: Their Organization and Activity in the Modern State*, trans. Barbara and Robert North (New York: John Wiley & Sons, 1963), p. 216; Sir Dingle Foot, *British Political Crises* (London: William Kimber, 1976), p. 18.

41. Mannheim, "The Problem of Generations," p. 297n; Karl Mannheim, "The Problem of Youth in Modern Society," in his *Diagnosis of Our Time* (New York: Oxford University Press, 1944), pp. 39-40; Klemens von Klemperer, *Germany's New Conservatism: Its History and Dilemma in the Twentieth Century* (Princeton: Princeton University Press, 1957), p. 44; Harold L. Poor, *Kurt Tucholsky and the Ordeal of Germany 1914-1935* (New York: Charles Scribner's Sons, 1968), p. 25.

42. Two interesting beginnings for the study of this process are: John Crittenden, "Aging and Political Participation," *The Western Political Quarterly* 16 (June 1963):323-31; John Crittenden, "Aging and Party Affiliation," *The Public Opinion Quarterly* 26 (Winter 1962):648-57. It is, however, difficult to avoid the conclusion that "the model of a regulated, and rather unchanging, series of age-graded passages of status is far too simple a model to be very useful for studying modern societies." Strauss, *Mirrors and Marks*, p. 134.

43. Paul R. Abramson, "Generational Change and the Decline of Party Identification in America: 1952-1974," *The American Political Science Review* 70 (June 1976):473. One author claims, mistakenly, that generations theory argues that "as the age-basis of commitment wanes, so will the commitment itself." Bennett M. Berger, "How Long is a Generation?" *The British Journal of Sociology* 11 (March 1960):17. On the contrary, the assumption made by a generational approach is that commitment is "conserved as a cohort ages." David Butler and Donald Stokes, *Political Change in Britain*, 2nd ed. (New York: St. Martin's Press, 1976), p. 42. If Berger's interpretation were correct, the study of youth movements could be separated from the study of long-term motivations for political action. Such separation would be unfortunate, but at the same time it would be a mistake to equate the study of youth movements with the study of political generations, since what really matters is the degree to which attitudes assumed in youth persist throughout the individual human lifetime. To assume that this degree is complete without further inquiry would be to accept generations theory as an act of faith, not reason.

44. Gabriel A. Almond and G. Bingham Powell, Jr., *Comparative Poli-*

tics: System, Process, and Policy (Boston: Little, Brown and Company, 1978), p. 79.

45. Butler and Stokes, *Political Change in Britain*, p. 40.

46. Paul R. Abramson, "Generational Change in American Electoral Behavior," *The American Political Science Review* 68 (March 1974):100; Clifford Adelman, *Generations: A Collage on Youth-cult* (Harmondsworth, Eng.: Penguin Books, 1973), p. 44.

47. Marvin Rintala, "The Two Faces of Compromise," *The Western Political Quarterly* 22 (June 1969):326-32.

48. Friedrich Nietzsche, *Schopenhauer as Educator*, trans. James W. Hillesheim and Malcolm R. Simpson, Chicago: Henry Regnery Company, 1965), p. 73; J. D. B. Miller, in *Political Studies* 9 (February 1961): 84; Vilho Niitemaa, "Jalmari Jaakkola," *Historiallinen Aikakauskirja*, 1964, pp. 2-3; Harold R. Isaacs, "Fathers and Sons and Daughters and National Development," in Samuels, ed., *Political Generations and Political Development*, p. 47; Samuel P. Huntington, in Samuels, ed., *Political Generations and Political Development*, p. 24.

49. Hans Gerth, "On the Passing of C. Wright Mills," *Berkeley Journal of Sociology* 7 (Spring 1962):2; A. P. Elkin, "Dean of Australian anthropologists," *International Social Science Journal* 25 (1973):13; Celso Furtado, "Adventures of a Brazilian economist," *International Social Science Journal* 25 (1973):33.

50. Joseph La Palombara in *The American Political Science Review* 71 (September 1977):1153.

51. In evaluating Mannheim's personal approach to the sociology of knowledge, of which generations theory is an important component, a perceptive critic implicitly suggested as much. Paul Kecskemeti, Introduction to Mannheim, *Essays on the Sociology of Knowledge*, p. 31. As an old man, another distinguished advocate of a generational approach confessed that "the basis of my philosophical thought" had been laid in his first book. Ortega y Gasset, *Man and People*, p. 42. Mannheim's own generational membership has been incorrectly identified by Kurt H. Wolff, ed., *From Karl Mannheim* (New York: Oxford University Press, 1971), pp. xii-xiii. Even though most studies of the sociology of knowledge ignore generations theory, it is clear that Mannheim intended the latter to be part of the former. Ibid., pp. xlix, li; Karl Mannheim, *Ideology and Utopia: An Introduction to the Sociology of Knowledge*, trans. Louis Wirth and Edward Shils (New York: Harcourt, Brace and Company, no date), pp. 270-76.

52. Allen Drury, *A Shade of Difference* (New York: Pocket Books, 1963), p. 429.

53. August Strindberg, *The Son of a Servant: The Story of the Evolution*

of a Human Being (1849-1867), trans. Evert Sprinchorn (New York: Double-day & Co., 1966), p. 75.

54. Plumb, *The First Four Georges*, p. 96.

55. T. Love Peacock, *Melincourt*, vol. II (London: J. M. Dent and Company, 1891), pp. 16-17.

56. Richard Rose, *Politics in England: An Interpretation* (Boston: Little, Brown and Company, 1964), p. 80.

57. Bryant M. Wedge, "Treatment of Idiosyncratic Adaptation in College Students," in *Psychosocial Problems of College Men*, ed. Bryant M. Wedge (New Haven: Yale University Press, 1958), p. 264; Paynter, *My Generation*, p. 15.

58. William James, *The Principles of Psychology*, vol. I (New York: Henry Holt and Company, 1890), p. 121; see also Ronald Blythe, *Akenfield: Portrait of an English Village* (Harmondsworth, Eng.: Penguin Books, 1975), p. 196.

59. James, *The Principles of Psychology*, vol. I, p. 122; George Santayana, *Persons and Places: The Background of My Life* (New York: Charles Scribner's Sons, 1964), pp. 8, 138-39, 156.

60. R. F. Delderfield, *To Serve Them All My Days* (New York: Simon and Schuster, 1972), p. 278.

61. Adolf Hitler, *Mein Kampf*, trans. Ralph Manheim, Boston: Houghton Mifflin Company, 1943), p. 67.

62. Ibid., p. 22.

63. Ernest Barker, *Age and Youth: Memories of Three Universities and Father of the Man* (London: Oxford University Press, 1953), p. 156; Cecil Gray, *Sibelius* (London: Oxford University Press, 1931), p. 64; Alfred Einstein, *A Short History of Music*, 4th ed. (New York: Vintage Books, 1962), p. 143; Furtado, "Adventures of a Brazilian Economist," p. 34; Miriam Rothschild in *The Sunday Times Magazine*, October 7, 1973, p. 105.

64. Kenneth D. Barkin, *The Controversy over German Industrialization 1890-1902* (Chicago: The University of Chicago Press, 1970), p. 10.

65. *The Autobiography of Nahum Goldmann: Sixty Years of Jewish Life*, trans. Helen Sebba (New York: Holt, Rinehart and Winston, 1969), p. 73.

66. Frank Brennand, *The Young Churchill* (London: New English Library, 1972), p. 87.

67. Mannheim's approach is, however, free of the particular weakness present in the assumption that each generation is born with certain characteristics, made by: José Ortega y Gasset, *The Modern Theme*, trans. James Cleugh (New York: Harper & Brothers, 1961), p. 15; Raley, *José Ortega y Gasset*, p. 88,

68. An author severely critical of a generational approach nevertheless

assumes that generations advocates refer to "the young child who is not in the labor market." Herbert H. Hyman, *Political Socialization: A Study in the Psychology of Political Behavior* (Glencoe, Ill.: The Free Press, 1959), p. 125. Hyman concludes that, compared with college students, "the younger child is not yet responsive to the impact of social change and is insulated from it by his home environment." Ibid., p. 131. Rather than contradicting a generational approach, Hyman's conclusion is entirely consistent with the latter. Indeed, Hyman's conclusion suggests that he should view generations theory as much more useful than he does.

69. David Easton and Robert D. Hess, "The Child's Political World," *Midwest Journal of Political Science* 6 (August 1962):236.

70. Fred I. Greenstein, "The Benevolent Leader: Children's Images of Political Authority," *The American Political Science Review* 54 (December 1960):940; Donald D. Searing, Joel J. Schwartz, and Alden E. Lind, "The Structuring Principle: Political Socialization and Belief Systems," *The American Political Science Review* 67 (June 1972):415-16, 431.

71. Hess and Torney, *The Development of Political Attitudes in Children*, p. 15.

72. Strindberg, *The Son of a Servant*, pp. 242-43.

73. David Easton and Jack Dennis, "The Child's Acquisition of Regime Norms: Political Efficacy," *The American Political Science Review* 61 (March 1967): 34n.

74. Jack Dennis in *The American Political Science Review* 60 (March 1966):117.

75. Mannheim, "The Problem of Generations," p. 300.

76. André Gide, *If It Die . . . an autobiography*, trans. Dorothy Bussy (New York: Vintage Books, 1957), p. 169.

77. Kyllikki Kallas, *Kolmastoista luku:romaani* (Helsinki: Kustannuso-sakeyhtiö Tammi, 1961), p. 112; Powell, *A Buyer's Market*, p. 14; Remarque, *Three Comrades*, p. 7.

78. Mary McCarthy, *The Groves of Academe* (New York: The New American Library, 1963), p. 208; William Logue, *Léon Blum: The Formative Years 1872-1914* (DeKalb: Northern Illinois University Press, 1973), p. 28. Even an otherwise unsympathetic observer conceded that "youth was the only time in which we learned anything." Marcel Proust, *Within a Budding Grove*, trans. C. K. Scott Moncrieff (New York: Vintage Books, 1970), p. 225.

79. Sachs, *Witches' Sabbath*, pp. 58-59; Normak Kiell, *The Universal Experience of Adolescence* (Boston; Beacon Press,1968), p. 25.

80. Waltari, *Isästä poikaan*, p. 222; Paustovsky, *The Story of a Life*, p. 42.

81. Waltari, *Isästä poikaan*, p. 510; Churchill, *My Early Life*, p. 60.

82. Ortega y Gasset, *Man and People*, pp. 161-62; James S. Davie, "Satisfaction and the College Experience," in Wedge, ed., *Psychosocial Problems of College Men*, pp. 17-18; Lifton, "Youth and History," p. 194; Keniston, "Social Change and Youth in America," p. 162; S. N. Eisenstadt, "Archetypal Patterns of Youth," *Daedalus*, Winter 1962, p. 30; Peter Blos, *On Adolescence: A Psychoanalytic Interpretation* (New York: The Free Press of Glencoe, 1962), pp. 136, 147; Private 19022 [Frederick Manning], *Her Privates We* (London: Peter Davies, 1930), p. 336; Sarah Grand, *The Heavenly Twins* (London: William Heinemann, 1894), p. 25.

83. Santayana, *Persons and Places*, p. 118.

84. Ibid., p. 151.

85. Väinö Linna, *Täällä Pohjantähden alla—toinen osa* (Porvoo: Werner Söderström Osakeyhtiö, 1960), p. 38.

86. Jussi Talvi, *Hyvä on elämä: Romaani* (Helsinki: Kustannusosakeyhtiö Otava, 1956), p. 193; Sachs, *Witches' Sabbath*, pp. 69, 158.

87. Jussi Talvi, *Yksi miljoonista:Romaani* (Helsinki: Kustannusosakeyhtiö Otava, 1959), p. 29; Paustovsky, *The Story of a Life*, p. 258.

88. Toivo Pekkanen, *Lapsuuteni* (Porvoo: Werner Söderström Osakeyhtiö, 1959), p. 215.

89. Waltari, *Isästä poikaan*, p. 84; Günter Grass, *Speak Out! Speeches, Open Letters, Commentaries*, trans. Ralph Manheim (New York: Harcourt, Brace & World, 1969), p. 55.

90. Alice S. Rossi, "Generational Differences in the Soviet Union," vol. I, mimeographed (Cambridge: Russian Research Center, Harvard University, 1954), p. 329. see also ibid., pp. 322-30.

91. George Santayana, *The Last Puritan: A Memoir in the Form of a Novel* (New York: Charles Scribner's Sons, 1961), p. 311.

92. Ibid., p. 318; T. M. Kivimäki, *Suomalaisen poliitikon muistelmat* (Porvoo: Werner Söderström Osakeyhtiö, 1965), pp. 23-24, 31; Alan Thomas, *A Life Apart* (London: Victor Gollancz Ltd., 1968), p. 26.

93. Tolstoy, *Childhood, Boyhood and Youth*, p. 218.

94. Waltari, *Isästä poikaan*, p. 221; Thomas Jones, *Lloyd George* (London: Oxford University Press, 1951), p. 8.

95. Tolstoy, *Childhood, Boyhood and Youth*, p. 139.

96. Otto Klineberg, "Reflections of an international psychologist of Canadian origin," *International Social Science Journal* 25 (1973):53; Neumann, *Permanent Revolution*, p. 236; Rose, *Politics in England*, p. 59; Gordon R. Lowe, *The Growth of Personality: from Infancy to Old Age* (Harmondsworth, Eng.: Penguin Books, 1972), pp. 159, 164.

97. Henry James, *A Small Boy and Others* (New York: Charles Scribner's Sons, 1962), pp. 49, 56-57; Herbert Read, *The Contrary Experience: autobiographies* (London: Faber and Faber, 1963), pp. 154, 200-201.

98. Paavo Rintala, *Mummoni ja Mannerheim: Romaani* (Helsinki: Kustannusosakeyhtiö Otava, 1960), p. 15. In this case, the youth took himself out of the society in which he had spent his childhood. Antisocial actions, however, are also social actions.

99. David Donald, *Charles Sumner and the Coming of the Civil War* (New York: Alfred A. Knopf, 1961), pp. 14-15.

100. Thomas A. Bailey, *Woodrow Wilson and the Great Betrayal* (Chicago: Quadrangle Books, 1963),. p. 13; Isaiah Berlin, *Karl Marx: His Life and Environment* (New York: Oxford University Press, 1959), p. 259; Rudolph Binion, *Defeated Leaders: The Political Fate of Caillaux, Jouvenel, and Tardieu* (New York: Columbia University Press, 1960), p. 138; Churchill, *My Early Life*, pp. 59, 200-201, 306, 370; *The Early Years of Alec Waugh* (New York: Farrar, Straus and Company, 1963), p. 138; Anthony Eden, *Another World, 1897-1917* (London: Allen Lane, 1976), p. 80; Karl Geiringer, *Brahms: His Life and Work*, 2nd ed. (Garden City, N.Y.: Doubleday & Company, 1961), pp. 26, 33, 35, 37; Jägerskiöld, *Nuori Mannerheim*, pp. 68-69, 182, 195, 207, 322; *A King's Story*, p. 77; Kivimäki, *Suomalaisen poliitikon muistelmat*, p. 29; Mead, *Blackberry Winter*, pp. 95, 101-2, 105, 109; *Paasikiven muistelmia sortovuosilta*, vol. II (Porvoo: Werner Söderström Osakeyhtiö, 1957), p. 214; Anthony Powell, *A Buyer's Market* (New York: Popular Library, 1976), pp. 227-28; Anthony Powell, *Hearing Secret Harmonies* (New York: Popular Library, 1976), p. 79; Santayana, *Persons and Places*, pp. 178-85, 195, 224-37; C. P. Snow, *Corridors of Power* (New York: Charles Scribner's Sons, 1964), pp. 37, 147; C. P. Snow, *Strangers and Brothers* (New York: Charles Scribner's Sons, 1962), p. 135; Charles Hamilton Sorley, *Marlborough and Other Poems* (Cambridge: at the University Press, 1922), p. 123; Igor Stravinsky, *An Autobiography* (New York: W. W. Norton & Company, 1962), pp. 17, 25; Barker, *Age and Youth*, p. 86.

101. Carl Schmitt, *The Concept of the Political*, trans. George Schwab (New Brunswick, N.J.: Rutgers University Press, 1976), 26, 28-29, 64, 67; George Schwab, *The Challenge of the Exception: An Introduction to the Political Ideas of Carl Schmitt between 1921 and 1936* (Berlin: Duncker & Humblot, 1970), pp. 51-55.

102. *The Early Years of Alec Waugh*, p. 138.

103. Mead, *Blackberry Winter*, p. 111; Priestley, *Margin Released*, pp. 71, 73.

104. Logue, *Léon Blum*, p. 89; Snow, *Corridors of Power*, p. 32.

105. H. H. Gerth and C. Wright Mills, eds., *From Max Weber: Essays in Sociology* (New York: Oxford University Press, 1958), p. 128.

106. Angus Campbell et al., *The American Voter* (New York: John Wiley & Sons, 1960), p. 148; Mark Benney, A. P. Gray, and R. H. Pear, *How People Vote: A Study of Electoral Behaviour in Greenwich* (London: Routledge and Kegan Paul Ltd., 1956), p. 106; Donald Chapman, "What Prospect for the Labour Party?" *The Political Quarterly* 25 (July-September 1954):211; Göran von Bonsdorff, *Studier rörande den moderna liberalismen i de nordiska länderna* (Lund: C. W. K. Gleerup, 1954), p. 247; Ruth Link, "A World Without Price-tags," *Sweden Now* 9 (1975):43; Mervin B. Freedman, "Studies of College Alumni," in *The American College: A Psychological and Social Interpretation of the Higher Learning*, ed. Nevitt Sanford (New York: John Wiley & Sons, 1962), pp. 857-58, 860, 864; Robert E. Lane and David O. Sears, *Public Opinion* (Englewood Cliffs, N.J.: Prentice-Hall, 1964), p. 31; Norval D. Glenn, "Aging, Disengagement, and Opinionation," *The Public Opinion Quarterly* 33 (Spring 1969):17-33; Norval D. Glenn and Michael Grimes, "Aging, Voting, and Political Interest," *American Sociological Review* 33 (August 1968): 568; Richard Aldington, *Life for Life's Sake: A Book of Reminiscences* (London: Cassell, 1968), p. 83; Herbert Read, *The Contrary Experience*, pp. 202, 206.

107. *The Autobiography of Nahum Goldmann*, p. 43; Kivimäki, *Suomalaisen poliitikon muistelmat*, p. 27; I. Deutscher, *Stalin: A Political Biography* (New York: Oxford University Press, 1949), p. 43; Sir Oswald Mosley, *My Life* (New Rochelle, N.Y.: Arlington House, 1972), pp. 91, 100; Violet Bonham Carter, *Winston Churchill: An Intimate Portrait* (New York: Harcourt, Brace & World, 1965), p. 67; Robert Rhodes James, *Churchill: A Study in Failure 1900-1939* (Harmondsworth, Eng.: Penguin Books, 1973), p. 444; Max Beloff, *Imperial Sunset: Volume I: Britain's Liberal Empire, 1897-1921* (New York: Alfred A. Knopf, 1970), pp. 12, 112; E. T. Raymond, *Mr. Lloyd George* (New York: George H. Doran Company, 1922), p. 316; Hubert Humphrey, interviewed in *Parade*, October 2, 1977, p. 10.

108. Snow, *Corridors of Power*, p. 284.

109. W. R. P. George, *The Making of Lloyd George* (London: Faber and Faber, 1976), p. 83.

110. Konrad Adenauer on "Meet the Press," April 16, 1961.

111. V. J. Sukselainen, "A Statesman's Life," *Finlandia Review* (Helsinki: The Finnish Foreign Trade Association, 1957), p. 35.

112. Hugh Dalton, *Towards the Peace of Nations: A Study in International Politics* (London: George Routledge & Sons, Ltd., 1928), p. ix.

113. John Viscount Morley, *On Compromise* (London: Macmillan & Co. Ltd., 1921), p. 1. This statement is remarkably similar to a novelist's per-

ception, involving recollection of political attitudes of student days: "I ought to confess that some of the thinking I did then was as clear and definite as anything I have ever done: and I settled a good many questions in a way that I should still maintain." C. P. Snow, *The Search* (New York: The New American Library, 1960), p. 44.

114. James Joll, *Three Intellectuals in Politics* (New York: Pantheon Books, 1969), pp. 21-22, 52, 56.

115. Ibid., p. xi.

116. Hans Kohn, *Living in a World Revolution: My Encounters with History* (New York: Simon and Schuster, 1970), p. 104.

Essay 2

The European War Generation of 1914-18

The temporal and spatial limits of a given historical experience define the size of the resulting political generation, just as the degree of uniqueness of that event determines the degree of difficulty that generation will have in communicating with earlier and later generations. In this sense the political generation created by World War I was a general European phenomenon.[1] It was neither worldwide nor confined to one or a few European nations. The limited nature of the war experience outside Europe meant that the war had far less impact on, say, American or Japanese youth than on European youth.[2] The enormous transformation of European society that the war involved meant, on the other hand, that World War I led to creation of a new political generation throughout Europe, in contrast to the relatively limited significance of, say, the Crimean or Franco-Prussian wars in this respect.

Those Europeans whose formative years, in whole or in part, occurred during 1914-18, especially those who actually fought in the trenches, were not all influenced in the same way, but they were nevertheless all decisively influenced by it. Their reactions to the war were often very different, depending upon their nationality, their class origins and aspirations, and, especially, personal wartime experiences.[3] It mattered whether a soldier had been taught to respect war as an act of national necessity or to detest it as exploitation of the international working class. It mattered even more whether that soldier fought in a victorious or a defeated army. In a real sense, however, the fact that they all experienced the war

in their formative years determined the attitudes toward politics—
for the rest of their lives—of those Europeans born between 1890
and 1900. For each of them the Great War remained "my war."[4]

In addition, whatever their personal reactions to the war, the
lives of the war generation were unavoidably tied together by the
problems that emerged for European society as a consequence of
World War I. Political integration, as well as political disintegration,
can take many forms, and the creation of a European war generation
was far more meaningful, although—given human mortality—less
lasting, to its members than many other forms of political community might have been. *E pluribus unum* can have more than one
meaning, and the war generation may have been more European
than nationalist. One of the most gifted members of the war generations, who was perhaps also the most brilliant politician of his
generation,[5] wrote of "the fundamental conception of European
union which animated the war generation."[6] At least for such
members of the war generation "all Europe is my home."[7] For such
members of the war generation the Great War was not so much a
war among nations as the first international civil war of modern
Europe, whose real analog was the Peloponnesian War.[8]

Whatever the role of nationalism in the origins of World War I,
the written remains of the war generation testify to an almost complete lack of nationalist sentiment in the trenches. Soldiers may or
may not have been dying for their nation, but they certainly did
not sing its praises with their dying lips. Those in the ranks, unlike
many of the political leaders at the Peace Conference, expressed
little feeling of hatred for their opponents on the other side of No
Man's Land.[9] Prisoners of war were well treated by their guards,[10]
so much so that those prisoners probably pitied their captors, who
still had to do battle.[11] Soldiers on one side could decline to take
prisoner unarmed soldiers of the other side,[12] and soldiers on that
other side also could allow their supposed enemies to escape being
taken prisoner.[13] The wounded and killed of both sides were treated
with enormous respect by both sides.[14] German medical corpsmen
could give preference to wounded British soldiers over wounded
German soldiers,[15] and healthy German soldiers could bury a British
soldier under a cross bearing the legend, in German: "Here rests the

brave English Captain."[16] The death of an enemy brought respect and grief, not triumph.[17] Indeed, it was not the killing of the enemy but—in a very precise sense—the sacrifice of one's own life that was the significant action in battle.[18]

It was soon apparent to those in the front lines that the picture of the enemy that nationalist propaganda had given was seriously distorted: "I remember well my comrades' looks of astonishment when we faced the Tommies in person in Flanders. After the very first days of battle the conviction dawned on each and every one of them that these Scotsmen did not exactly jibe with the pictures they had seen fit to give us in the comic magazines and press dispatches."'[19] Soldiers in the trenches had genuine pity for their opponents.[20] The elation of capturing the latter's trenches was brief:

It seemed marvellous, for the moment! All ours—all these German trenches. Caliban Support, Calf Avenue, Calf Reserve. But, stay—even now a pity looks one in the face, for these trenches are mostly mere hedges of brush-wood, hurdles, work for a sheepfold, with a shallow ditch behind; and they have been taking our weeks of gunfire in these![21]

Across the barbed wire one did not see inhuman beasts but "More poor devils like yourselves / Waiting to be killed by you."[22] When this wait was over, there was little pleasure for those who had shot first, who realized: "Perhaps he was the only son. . . ."[23]

The greatest literary achievement of the war generation, Wilfred Owen's "Strange Meeting," is a description of such a meeting of two members of Owen's generation in Hell. The final draft of this poem includes the line: "I am the enemy you killed, my friend." In an earlier draft, Owen had been even more explicit: "I was a German conscript, and your friend."[24] Another of the literary masterpieces flowing from the formative experiences of the war generation is dedicated: "TO THE ENEMY FRONT-FIGHTERS WHO SHARED OUR PAINS AGAINST WHOM WE FOUND OURSELVES BY MISADVENTURE."[25] In such circumstances, threats and menacing gestures were meaningless, and resignation to one's fate was every-thing.[26] It was possible for an educated British soldier to sing a favorite German song shortly before dying in battle,[27] and for educated soldiers on both sides to enjoy Nietzsche, Keats, and Rimbaud.[28] Less learned serenades could be heard across No Man's Land,[29] and the same, and equally necessary, village water pump could be shared by both sides.[30]

Since it was not yet the world of the permanent purge and the concentration camp, it was still possible to respect the professional competence of the enemy.[31] At a mess dinner of British pilots a toast was drunk to "von Richthofen, our most worthy enemy."[32] It was also still possible to admire the enemy's bravery,[33] his sense of humor,[34] and, above all, his human worth.[35] Those in the trenches perceived that the only distinguishing characteristic of the enemy was that his uniform was of a different color,[36] and even this difference was not really distinguishable. As a Frenchman later recalled of November 1916 on the Somme plains: "There were no more horizon-blue or feldgrau . . . greatcoats: The wheatland, whose acres had cost so many lives, had become our common uniform."[37] It was even possible to respect the enemy more than oneself. A German soldier guarding Russians in a prisoner-of-war camp observed of his prisoners: "They are more human and more brotherly towards one another, it seems to me, than we are."[38] A German sailor concluded: "I would rather be a slave to the English than a German sailor."[39] The succinct conclusion on what was ostensibly the other side, was, nevertheless: "even Huns are men."[40]

Indeed, sometimes the enemy from the battlefield seemed preferable to the supporter on the home front. In late 1914 C. H. Sorley, who was to die in battle a few months later, wrote a letter that does not suggest he died for his nation:

England—I am sick of the word. In training to fight for England, I am training to fight for that deliberate hypocrisy, that terrible middle-class sloth of outlook and appalling "imaginative indolence" that has marked us out from generation to generation. . . . Indeed I think that after the war all brave men will renounce their country and confess that they are strangers and pilgrims on the earth. . . . I might have been giving my mind to fight against Sloth and Stupidity: instead, I am giving my body (by a refinement of cowardice) to fight against the most enterprising nation in the world.[41]

In the summer of 1918, while on medical leave in the United Kingdom, Wilfred Owen wrote in a personal letter: "I wish the Boche

would have the pluck to come right in and make a clean sweep of
the pleasure boats, and the promenaders on the Spa, and all the
stinking Leeds and Bradford war-profiteers now reading *John Bull*
on Scarborough Sands."[42] British soldiers refused to sing "God
Save the King"[43] and "didn't care who won as long as we could get
the war over."[44] The same sentiment was articulated with perfect
clarity by a Russian soldier who saw "rivers of blood all because of
criminals and idiots," "these bombastic Wilhelms and foolish
Nicholases. And the grasping businessmen. Some are cretins, the
others are black rascals."[45] This distaste for one's fellow nationals
extended to one's own generals, who were blamed for having
prevented the fraternization of Christmas 1914 becoming the
normal state of affairs.[46] The desire was real to "push the generals
and the politicans into this filth—nose first!"[47] Quite typical of
reality is the feeling of a fictional young British officer: "Christ . . .
sometimes I think I'd sooner shoot a general than a Jerry."[48] A real
young British officer revealed that his men refused to shoot German
soldiers "though ordered to do so."[49] A British member of the war
generation later observed of the interwar years: "In those days the
front-line soldiers of 1914- to 1918 formed a secret society which
knew neither rank nor nationality."[50] In Weimar Germany, a former
soldier said of those who had been permanent civilians: "We would
get along better with any Tommy, with any frontline Froggy, than
with them."[51] Relying on precisely this assumption, the British
Legion conducted its own independent foreign policy, trying, for
instance, to cement good relations with German veterans' associa-
tions, especially after 1933.[52] Many British veterans supported
Hitler's occupation of the Rhineland.[53] In 1938 George VI offered
to write to Adolf Hitler "as one ex-serviceman to another."[54] George's
older brother, as Prince of Wales, had encouraged exchanges of
visits between British and German veterans.[55]

Just as some Marxists were disillusioned in 1914 when French and
German workers fought each other, some members of the war
generation were disillusioned when members of their generation
fought each other: "But think of it! A generation annihilated! A
generation of hope, of faith, of will, strength, ability, so hypnotised
that they have shot down one another, though over the whole
world [*sic*] they all had the same purpose!"[56] What Remarque

forgot in his idealized picture was that without the Great War there
would have been no war generation, and therefore nothing to
idealize. If, as Heraclitus observed, war is the father of all things,
it was certainly the father of the war generation.

If war created the war generation, it also almost destroyed its
creation. The voices missing from a roll call of the war generation
after 1918 were many.[57] World War I was truly the Great War for
Europe. Ten million soldiers could lament:

For of my glee might many men have laughed,
And of my weeping something had been left,
Which must die now.[58]

The major battles of World War I were above all battles of human
material, in distinct contrast to those of World War II.[59] At Passchendaele, "Haig, who ought to have gone up there himself or gone
home, was slicing my whole generation into sausage meat held
above a swill bucket."[60] Alternatively, Haig, a "stupid sod,"[61]
"should have been hung, drawn and quartered for what he did on
the Somme."[62] At Verdun, a hundred square miles' gain for the
German Imperial Army has been purchased at the cost of half a
million casualties on *each* side. Even such losses were surpassed by
those on the Somme—where for all practical purposes the entire
volunteer, preconscription British Army was wiped out,[63] on the
Eastern Front, and during the last desperate gamble by the German
Army in the spring of 1918. In the battle of Langemarck a thousand
volunteers, all of them active in the German youth movement,
were killed in one afternoon in an otherwise insignificant skirmish
around a Flanders hill. One of every four *Wandervogel* was dead
by 1918.[64] The significance of this fact did not escape a soldier in
the German Army whose career prospects before 1914 had seemed
far less promising than those of the *Wandervogel*.[65]

The impact on European politics of the loss of millions of members of the war generation can hardly be exaggerated. Particularly
important was the loss of potential political leaders, but it was not
only leaders who were missing in European politics after 1918, but
followers as well. The most striking case was undoubtedly France.
Only half of her sons returned home.[66] The gaps that 1914-18 left in
the vulnerable French population structure moved year by year up

the age pyramid, but were never filled. The French total population loss, adding killed and natality loss from the consequent depressed birth rate, was 3.33 million persons.[67] In the years of German rearmament under Hitler the French population problem was most severe. From 1936 to 1940 the annual call-up of French conscripts fell from 240,000 to 120,000—one-fifth of that in 1914. Between 1930 and 1940 the number of marriages in France dwindled by half, and after 1934 the annual number of deaths actually exceeded that of births.[68] In this context, General Gamelin's reluctance in 1939-40 to risk another Verdun is perhaps understandable, if not particularly praiseworthy. France could not have survived the sacrifice of another war generation.[69] Whether the war generation of 1914-18 would have given its united blessing to French policy in 1939-40 is, however, uncertain.

Many members of the war generation who died in 1914-18 were immensely gifted, in accordance with Sophocles's argument in the *Philoctetes*.[70] It was entirely true, as British soldiers sang, that "Some have gone west / Best of the Best."[71] The missing voices of the war generation included many of the bravest.[72] The cowards lived to fight again another day, and there was considerable truth in the lines written by one of the most courageous surviving members of the war generation in the autumn of 1939: "They were the noblest of our strain / Those friends of ours who died."[73]

Some of those who died so young were clearly possessed of a vocation for politics.[74] Later they were sorely missed when it came time for their generation to assume positions of political leadership.[75] In inevitable consequence, pre-1914 generations were able to cling to power in Britain, as elsewhere, unusually long.[76] Some idea of the impact of this loss can be gained from the fate of young members of the British ruling class, educated at the prestige public schools and Oxford and Cambridge.

One of three recent graduates of Charterhouse died.[77] Of the forty-six boys in one house at Haileybury in 1913, twenty were dead within five years.[78] Of the Balliol Scholars and Exhibitioners of their year only Harold Macmillan and one of his coevals survived 1918.[79] New College, at Oxford, lost more than the intake of three whole years.[80] More than four thousand Sandhurst cadets lost their lives in the Great War,[81] and Britain lost 9 percent of its adult males under forty-five years of age.[82] Not all those who died were budding members of the British establishment. A survivor of Gallipoli later related that of those sixty fellow-townsmen with whom he had left for war, only three returned.[83] Britain was literally bled white.[84] Already after Loos in 1915 it was appropriate for a soldier to recall the seven glasses he and his comrades had needed for convivial pleasure and to add starkly, "Now we only call for three."[85] It was only a slight exaggeration to state: "All my Young England fell to-day in fight."[86] The surviving members of the war generation felt distinctly guilty, as if their survival could only be explained by ignoble motives,[87] and one of them was candid enough to state that "those of us who are left know that we are the runts."[88] These survivors perhaps agreed with the harsh judgment of Priam upon his remaining sons after the deaths of Hector, Mestor, and Troilus: "Ares slew them, and all these cowards are left—the liars and the dancers, masters of choral dancing, thieves of rams and kids at home."[89]

Whatever Priam's surviving sons were like, those members of the war generation still alive after war's end found it difficult to be frivolous. In 1917 a young poet, Kurt Schulze, wrote of his fellow German soldiers: "When they return home they will no longer want to dance . . . and their faith is broken."[90] This was an accurate prediction, which matched precisely what a British soldier wrote in his diary in the same year after the death of yet another friend in battle: "I begin to feel that the dance is already over and that it is time to go."[91] In the rich imagery of the war generation it is the dance of death that is predominant.[92]

In many respects the surviving members of the war generation deserved after 1918 the adjectives they applied to themselves— lost,[93] shattered,[94] bankrupt,[95] rootless.[96] They were literally "something left over from the war."[97]

We don't want to take the world by storm. We are fleeing. We fly from ourselves. From our life. We were eighteen and had begun to love life and the world; and we had to shoot it to pieces. The first bomb, the first explosion, burst in our hearts. We are cut off from activity, from striving, from progress. We believe in such things no longer, we believe in the war.[98]

There was, of course, considerable justification for this escapism.[99] Many of these men retreated into literature, religion, business, daydreams, alcohol, self-pity[100]—anything but responsible political action. The result of the political socialization process was for many of these survivors a profound aversion to politics. In a very real sense many of these survivors were just as much war casualties as those who never returned.[101] To be "heartless and hopeless and lifeless"[102] was no happy fate. To be left with "a profound and cynical discouragement, a shrinking horror of the human race,"[103] was not much better. This kind of reaction to World War I received its classic statement in the poetry of Edmund Blunden.[104] In such circumstances it seemed reasonable to ask: "What mercy is it I should live and move / If haunted ever by war's agony?"[105]

Restlessness was very common among surviving members of the war generation after 1918.[106] The symbol of this restlessness was, appropriately enough, the most prestigious member of the war generation, the Prince of Wales.[107] This restlessness was no doubt due in part to recognition of the fact that postwar careers had been postponed for many years.[108] Economic conditions and governmental policies were not always helpful to integration of returned veterans, many of them untrained in peacetime occupations, into economic life.[109] A British soldier later related: "I had only two Christmases at work between 1919 and 1939."[110]

Perhaps even more important, however, was the realization that the relatively peaceful and in many ways satisfying nineteenth century was gone forever:

Any intelligent European born, let us say, after 1904 reached the teens in what he or she knew to be a dangerous and cruel world. But if you were born in 1894, as I was, you suddenly saw a great jagged crack in the looking-glass. After that your mind could not escape from the idea of a world that ended in 1914, and another that began about 1919, with a wilderness of smoke and fury, outside sensible time, lying between them.[111]

The past seemed separated from the present "by thousands of miles and millions of years," and that past was a civilization "as dead as Nineveh's."[112] The response of many members of the war generation to this realization was to retreat from the new world that was being born, and even to deny its existence. Sometimes this reaction went so far as to suggest that the war had never taken place.[113] This suggestion, of course, was merely the mirror image of the suggestion

that the war was the only reality.[114] Symbolic of this reaction was
the British poet Ivor Gurney, gassed and wounded in 1917. Gurney
died in 1937 in a mental hospital, where he had continued to write
war poetry, convinced that the war was still going on.[115] Since the
Great War had lasted long enough to become an institution,[116]
this was perhaps sanity in a world of madmen.

Above all, many members of the war generation wanted to stay
out of politics, for it had been politics that led to 1914.[117] Whether
or not the war generation was lost in every sense of that term, many
of its surviving members were lost to political life.[118] In David
Lloyd George's famous "khaki" election in December 1918, only
one out of every four Britishers still in the armed forces voted.[119] In
some parts of the British Army, soldiers burned their absentee
ballots.[120] This was not surprising in that politicians had been
objects of contempt among soldiers throughout the war. Although
professional politicians generally are respected in Britain, in the
trenches British soldiers sang of a member of the House of Com-
mons comfortably legislating about irrelevant matters "While the
victims of his passions/Trudge on in mud and slime."[121] The game
of politics had little appeal for those for whom life had not been a
game—except of chance.[122] To resume a civilian habit of mind was
no easy task.[123] The only certainty many members of the war generation possessed about their vocation was that it was not politics.
An observant teacher later wrote of those students who entered
New College, Oxford, in 1919: "Only in the realm of politics was
the harvest sparse and thin. I do not remember a statesman or
politician who grew in that green field."[124] One of those soldiers
who returned from the war to study at New College in 1919 verified
this observation.[125] Many of his coevals "had a mind to lead a life
untouched by violence, and thought of our old studies."[126] One of
them, in a diary entry in 1918, articulated this kind of reaction to
the war: "I hate mobs—they fight and kill, build filthy cities and
make horrid dins."[127] A few weeks later, the same soldier drew in
his diary what seemed to him the logical conclusion:

And they are magnificently brave, English and German alike. But simply
because we are united into a callous inhuman association called a State,
and because a State is ruled by politicians whose aim (and under the cir-

cumstances their duty) is to support and maintain the life and sovereignty of this monster, life and hope are denied and sacrificed.[128]

If the absence of the missing voices of the war generation made inevitable the continued power of pre-1914 leaders, the continued rejection of politics after 1918 by many surviving members of the war generation doubly assured that power of older generations of leaders who had "learned nothing from the war, and forgot nothing."[129] Power was still in the hands of "the old men who had watched and waited from a safe distance,"[130] the very men who had been "the instigators and promoters of war."[131] Between the established political leaders and the members of the war generation there was

a dark screen of horror and violation: the knowledge of the reality of war. Across that screen I could not communicate. Nor could any of my friends who had had the same experience. We could only stand on one side, like exiles in a strange country.[132]

This retreat from politics by many members of the war generation was important in another respect, however: It made more significant the emergence and more likely the rise to power of political movements of the extreme right wing created by other members of the war generation. These latter, who numbered perhaps one hundred thousand in all of Europe, were men who entered politics as an inferior substitute for the trenches. They were militant irregulars, at war with the old bourgeois society[133] as well as with Communism. They were "full of disgust and revulsion at bourgeois cowardice and shilly-shallying."[134] They fought simply for the joy of fighting. They rejected the politics of compromise for the politics of violence. For them compromise was surrender to the enemy. The most powerful member of the war generation admitted the possibility that any political movement might suffer inner decay, but added:

I believe that the present generation, properly led, will more easily master this danger. It has experienced various things which had the power somewhat to strengthen the nerves of those who did not lose them entirely. In future days the Jew will certainly continue to raise a mighty uproar in his newspapers. . . . But I believe that this will bother us younger men less than our fathers. A thirty-centimeter shell has always hissed more loudly than a thousand Jewish newspaper vipers—so let them hiss![135]

For these militant irregulars politics was merely the continuation of war by other means. It was in war that they discovered politics was their vocation.[136] In October 1939, Adolf Hitler correctly stated: "We National Socialists once came from the war, from the experience of war. Our world ideal developed in war; now, if necessary, it will prove itself."[137]

Such a reaction was the least common among members of the war generation, but it was politically significant because most of the important leaders of the interwar extreme right-wing movements throughout Europe came from these militant members of the war generation.[138] In Germany, almost every major Nationalist Socialist leader had been born between 1890 and 1900.[139] These German members of the war generation included Hermann Goering, Rudolf Hess, Joseph Goebbels, Heinrich Himmler, Joachim von Ribbentrop, Robert Ley, Otto Dietrich, Walther Darré, and Alfred Rosenberg. The only significant leader of the National Socialist party not born between 1890 and 1900 was Adolf Hitler himself, born in 1889, but Hitler clearly was a member of the war generation nonetheless.

Hitler identified himself with the war generation in the second sentence of Mein Kampf, and this identification was entirely accurate. The greatest experience of Hitler's life was his participation in World War I.[140] He later recalled the beginning of the war: "To me those hours seemed like a release from the painful feelings of my youth. Even today I am not ashamed to say that, overpowered by stormy enthusiasm, I fell down on my knees and thanked Heaven from an overflowing heart for granting me the good fortune of being permitted to live at this time."[141] On August 4, 1914, he received permission, as an Austrian subject, to enlist in a Bavarian regiment: "My joy and gratitude knew no bounds. . . . for me, as for every German, there now began the greatest and most unforgettable time of my earthly existence. Compared to the events of this gigantic struggle, everything past receded to shallow nothingness."[142] This comparison was quite apt, since before 1914 Hitler's life had been full of shallow nothingness. Not only had he been apolitical before 1914,[143] but before 1914 his personality had not appeared in the form that the world eventually came to know so well.[144] Indeed, Adolf Hitler was nothing in 1914. If it had not been for World War I Hitler would never have risen from the Homes for the Homeless where he lived when able to pay the modest daily rent. More important, if it had not been for World War I German society would never have gotten into a situation where it would have needed, much less accepted, a foreign national who came from Skid Row as its saviour. There can be no reasonable doubt that it was World War I that raised Hitler to the position of absolute ruler of tens of millions of Europeans.

War had been the fundamental experience of the entire war generation during the most impressionable years of its members.[145] What was distinctive about the militant irregulars in the war generation was the degree of pleasure they derived from this experience.[146] For them the Great War was "only a salutary blood-letting."[147] Appropriately, the father of the theater of cruelty was a member of the war generation.[148] More than one member of the war generation "could speak with authority about the death of values because he had been present at their slaughter in the trenches."[149] These militant irregulars throughout Europe shared the response to the war of a young Finnish officer who had fought as a volunteer in the German army on the Eastern Front:

I acknowledge that I am one of those who sees good as well as evil in the war. It was a storm over the old Europe, that violently shook its nations, which were sinking into the softness of excessive culture. That which was weak or rotten disintegrated or perished. But a healthy tree, even when bruised, rises again out of the turmoil of the storm. With a broken top and with branches stripped bare it sinks its roots twice deeper and again pushes forth new buds. Soon it stands more erect than before, spreading a new stronger crown of leafy branches. . . . Even though millions fell and one generation sank into misery, it means no more in the thousand-years' life of nations than a floating cloud in the summer sky. Every manly act and willingly carried sacrifice that purely rose to the surface from amidst torrents of blood and crimes is immortal, for it gathers together all who confess the obligation of the past, to build the future of their race.[150]

The only society these militant members of the war generation both knew and approved was military. After World War I was over, they joined military formations like the Free Corps movement, the

Black *Reichswehr*, and finally the National Socialist or other extreme right-wing parties.[151] Their political structures throughout Europe were constructed on the leadership principle of military organizations. The army was the vanguard of the nation, and therefore it seemed entirely logical for one militant member of the war generation to conclude: "France was fashioned by the sword."[152] Life without the use of force was inconceivable, for force "is the prerequisite of movement and the midwife of progress."[153] To these militant members of the war generation the sword was the only law.[154] Violence became the ultimate sanction.[155] Might was equated with right,[156] and brutality was a customary and effective weapon in their strategy of terror. Respect for human life was at an absolute minimum among these militant irregulars.[157] For them patriotism meant "wearing a uniform again, becoming a colonel, and once more sending people to death."[158] As Hitler demonstrated in 1934, this lack of respect for human life applied to friends as well as foes.

Politics was for militant members of the war generation a real part of warfare, actual and potential, rather than a means to establish domestic tranquility or international peace. All that counted was obedience, success, and conquest. Perpetual war, not perpetual peace, appealed to those who were never at peace with themselves or with the world.[159] They repudiated the values of civil society and dedicated themselves to permanent revolution. In revolutionary Berlin at the end of World War I one of the defenders of the Republic said: "I want to have a weapon in my hand again. . . . Without a rifle a man isn't a man at all. That's why I joined, if you want to know . . . if we go about it the right way, the war can go on for ever."[160]

A leading member of *Action Française* later recalled that serving in the trenches had "filled my soul with a holy joy."[161] Another militant member of the war generation compared no man's land to "the Gethsemane in which Christ prayed that He might be relieved of the necessity for immolating Himself and then, in communion with God, discovered the peace that is the fruit of negating the objective self."[162] It is important to recognize, however, that this positive reaction towards the war was not confined to the relatively few militant irregulars. Many other members of the war generation shared this romantic conception of the war.[163] That peace was a

time of meanness and war was a time of nobility,[164] even of purifi-
cation,[165] was a common conclusion. The front line could be a
"place of enchantment,"[166] and one could be happy before, during,
and after battle.[167]

An important reason for happiness in the trenches was that class
lines were much less distinct there than elsewhere. Two songs of
British soldiers depicted this clearly:

The grub it was skimp with the ole sweats.
But if rashuns was small 'twas the same for us all. . . .[168]
. . . But here there's no distinction 'twixt Kensington and Bow,
We're comrades in the dug-out, all equals in the dug-out. . . .[169]

The *Gemeinschaft*[170] of the trenches, in which the class consciousness
of civilian life was generally reduced and often obliterated, attracted
most members of the war generation very much indeed.[171] In veterans'
organizations during the interwar decades distinctions of former
rank were meaningless.[172] It was, of course, not only in World War
I that the imminence of death reduced the significance of social
origins.[173]

Not all members of the war generation felt sufficiently purified
by their participation in World War I. Many responded to their
war experience by determining to create a new and better world. If
bad politics had caused the war, the solution was not to retreat
from politics, but to reform politics so such a war could never
recur. Promises had been made to fallen enemies:

Comrade . . . to-day you, to-morrow me. But if I come out of it, comrade,
I will fight against this, that has struck us both down; from you, taken life—
and from me?—Life also. I promise you, comrade. It shall never happen
again.[174]

Promises had also been made to one's self:

Standing there looking over the carnage-strewn morass, the need rose in
me to dedicate my pen to the portrayal of war as in itself it was; to expose the
popular, conventional idea of war. The politicians in their Whitehall
offices, the manufacturers pocketing their dividends, the publicists and the
apologists of war mouthing their telling periods must be made to face the

Gorgon; too many people were doing well out of the war; the common man was being exploited for their gain and glory. Never again, I vowed, never, never again. The young men of my generation must see to that.[175]

For such members of the war generation, their war had indeed been the war to end all wars,[176] and their hero was, perhaps predictably, Woodrow Wilson.[177] For them, the purpose of the war, as a British soldier wrote in a poem "To Germany" shortly before he was killed in action, had been to achieve a peace in which "we may view again / With new-won eyes each other's truer form."[178] Simply put, the hope of these members of the war generation was that human beings would learn "to love widely."[179] Given this hope, Article 231 of the Treaty of Versailles, holding Germany entirely responsible for the human and material losses of the Great War, was hardly likely to be viewed as just by even those members of the war generation who had fought in victorious armies.[180] Considering that, for instance, David Lloyd George rejected a request for participation in the Peace Conference by the British National Federation of Discharged and Demobilized Sailors and Soldiers,[181] the peace treaty was hardly likely to satisfy those who had fought the war and had greeted the Armistice with the question: "What will be the result of the ultimate peace if hatred cannot be sublimated?"[182]

Much of the effort of those who took up the pen instead of the sword was directed towards teaching other members of their generation never again to "think of war as anything but a vile, if necessary, evil."[183] Many went further than this, however, and argued that war was not only vile but unnecessary. For them, peace was the highest of all values. They were in fact pacifists.[184] They believed that "no peace can be worse than this bloody stupidity"[185] and that, as Isaac Rosenberg wrote in a letter, "nothing can justify war."[186] Their commitment was clear: "Above all, never, never again could there be, never must there be, another war."[187] They returned from the trenches "in a spirit of crusade, resolved to ensure that the crime of war would never be reenacted."[188] They had to put an end to war "no matter what it cost."[189] That cost, they recognized, included the fact that "I'd never fight for my country again."[190] They were the heirs of Wilfred Owen, who in 1917, in a letter from a military hospital in France, had written:

Already I have comprehended a light which never will filter into the dogma of any national church: namely, that one of Christ's essential commands was: Passivity at any price! Suffer dishonour and disgrace, but never resort to arms. Be bullied, be outraged, be killed; but do not kill. . . . Christ is literally in "no man's land." There men often hear His voice: Greater love hath no man than this, that a man lay down his life for a friend. Is it spoken in English only and French? I do not believe so. Thus you see how pure Christianity will not fit in with pure patriotism.[191]

They were also the heirs of Richard Stumpf, who had written in his diary on Good Friday 1918:

The spirit of Good Friday becomes especially meaningful when one reflects that Germany's youth has sacrificed its best years solely to destroy and kill men, the creations and images of God. In place of a single Calvary, our generation has millions of them.[192]

The reaction of these pacifists to 1914 had been far from favorable.[193] They hoped ardently for release from war, not just for themselves,[194] but for their entire generation: "O Star of Peace, rise swiftly in the East / That from such slaying men may be released."[195] Not all their words were prayerful, however, and these members of the war generation could curse their own weapons[196] and demand a return of their own humanity: "We want to be men again, not war machines!"[197] Their horror of war was lasting,[198] but they did not stop there. They wanted to build "a city of peace on the wastes of war."[199] They entered politics to work for "the salvation, not the destruction of humanity."[200] During the interwar decades, as well as later, the surviving members of the war generation who shared this reaction turned to collective security in the form of the League of Nations or the United Nations organization, or to disarmament, or even to both simultaneously.[201] Their hopes, of course, were frustrated—perhaps because of the inherent contradiction in being "against war but for collective security, for pacifism but against giving way to threats"[202] but also perhaps because of their own tragic flaw.[203] Tragic flaws, as Aristotle tells us, are the characteristics of tragic heroes.

It has been observed that there is polyphony among generations.[204] It is equally true that every generation speaks out with more than one voice—there is also polyphony within each generation. The different kinds of reactions to World War I are evidence of the different voices, what Karl Mannheim termed *generation units*, which together constituted a generation precisely because they were oriented towards each other, even if only to fight one another.[205] The responses of different members of the war generation to their experiences in battle were quite diverse. Some were so impressed by the war that they determined such a war should never recur. Others were so impressed by the war that they determined such warfare should be permanent. Still others were so impressed by the war that they determined never again to become involved with a human race that could be so brutal.

It is worth noting, however, that these different voices within the war generation were far more capable of communicating with each other than with members of older or younger, prewar or postwar, generations.[206] The internal communication of the war generation was considerably more effective than was communciation with those who had been either too old or too young to fight in World War I. The members of the war generation had learned to speak a common language based upon a community of experience,[207] and its members felt, probably correctly, that they possessed a secret that could never be communicated to others.[208]

None of the voices of the war generation was meaningful without the presence of the others. Least of all were the surviving voices meaningful without omnipresent missing voices. The different voices of the war generation were eloquent evidence for Karl Mannheim's argument: "The dynamic-antinomical unity of an epoch consists in the fact that polar opposites in an epoch always interpret their world in terms of one another, and that the various and opposing political orientations only become really comprehensible if viewed as so many different attempts to master the same destiny and solve the same social and intellectual problems that go with it."[209] In this respect the European war generation of 1914-18 resembled other war generations:

I see two other figures, not such constant landmarks throughout our childhood, but going back to very early days and then disappearing. These figures, contrasting so violently one with the other, are nevertheless bound together: they belong precisely to the same epoch, and their antithesis is so strong as almost to represent a likeness, one of them was Sir Henry Pennell, a magnificent old soldier, brave and handsome in his old age, gay, even when he suffered, and altogether charming, who had earned great distinction in the Crimean War; the other was "Old Charles," a deserter from the same conflict.[210]

Communications problems exist for all generations, but perhaps most strongly for war generations. Of all the many kinds of experiences men can share, which unite them with some men and divide them from others, the brotherhood of arms is the most unforgettable. None of the voices of the war generation could ever speak without a very heavy accent from the trenches: "In fifty years I have never been able to rid myself of the obsession with No Man's Land and the unknown world beyond it."[211] Their political and physical lives would end together. The Great War remained the central experience of both these lives.[212] It remains true that "We have the war in our bones still . . . and we'll never get it out again!"[213] In 1964 a British member of the war generation revisited Ypres, and spoke for his coevals of many nations: "I live in England but my heart is out here."[214] Another Britisher regularly visited the Somme, even in old age: "I try to be there on 1 July. I go out and, at 7:30 A.M., I stand at the exact spot where we went over the top in 1916."[215] The restlessness survived as long as did the war generation: "I still see those years as a time radiant with gleams and intimations, and the rest of life as one long journey further from the east."[216] The variations on the theme were several, but the entire membership of the war generation could agree: "Twenty million of us . . . are what we are because, in that war, we were soldiers."[217] All could understand the statement of one: "we bleed, we bleed to death, until we join the rest of our generation."[218]

NOTES

1. C. Day Lewis, ed., *The Collected Poems of Wilfred Owen* (New York: New Directions, 1964), pp. 108, 129; Henry Williamson, *The Golden Virgin* (London: Macdonald, 1966), p. 257. The only exceptions were in neutral states. A soldier in a neutral army later recalled that "we never got

to learn anything about how to handle any weapon." Gösta Lundvall, "Nothing Lives Forever," in Sture Källberg, *Report from a Swedish Village*, trans. Angela Gibbs (Harmondsworth, Eng.: Penguin Books, 1972), p. 15. The absence of a war generation in Sweden surely explains significantly Swedish political stability since 1918.

2. For moving but unpersuasive attempts to construct an American segment of the war generation, see S. L. A. Marshall, Introduction to Gene Smith, *Still Quiet on the Western Front: Fifty Years Later* (New York: William Morrow & Company, 1965); Frederick A. Pottle, "Creed Not Annulled," in *Promise of Greatness: The War of 1914-1918*, ed. George A. Panichas (New York: The John Day Company, 1968), pp. 359-62; Amos Wilder, "At the Nethermost Piers of History: World War I, a View from the Ranks—For Jules Deschamps," in Panichas, ed., *Promise of Greatness*, pp. 345-57; René Naegelen, "Recollections," in Panichas, ed., *Promise of Greatness*, p. 179; Norbert Wiener, *Ex-Prodigy: My Childhood and Youth* (Cambridge: The M.I.T. Press, 1972), pp. 217, 294. It has been argued that generational differences are greater in the United States than in Europe. Samuel P. Huntington, "Paradigms of American Politics: Beyond the One, the Two, and the Many," *Political Science Quarterly* 89 (March 1974): 23. In view of the enormous social, economic, and political traumas through which Europe has passed in the twentieth century, this argument seems strained at best. Probably only the Civil War and the Depression that began in 1929 have divided Americans from each other in such a significant way as World War I divided Europeans from each other. A solid case could perhaps be made in generational terms for the impact of World War II on the United States. Thomas Carr, of Plymouth, Michigan, put that case best while visiting the graveyard of American soldiers killed at Omaha Beach: "It's our generation buried here. I was in the war in Japan." *Boston Sunday Globe*, May 21, 1978, p. B16.

3. "But if you are to understand what I may call the battle-psychology of a man . . . you must not ignore particular incidents. For in this respect the lives of soldiers are not uniform; though they may live in the same regiment and fight in the same battles, the experiences which matter come to them diversely—to some crowded and overwhelming, to others by kind and delicate degrees. And so do their spirits develop." A. P. Herbert, *The Secret Battle*, 9th ed. (London: Methuen & Co., Ltd., 1949), p. 71; see also Will Paynter, *My Generation* (London: George Allen & Unwin Ltd., 1972), p. 10. Wars are fought in, by, for, and against groups of human beings, but soldiers die alone.

4. Ronald Blythe, *Akenfield: Portrait of an English Village* (Harmondsworth, Eng.: Penguin Books, 1975), p. 48.

5. J. B. Priestley, "Decade of Dreamers," *Books and Bookmen* 20 (July 1975):26.

6. Sir Oswald Mosley, *My Life* (New Rochelle, N. Y.: Arlington House, 1972), p. 384; see also ibid., p. 382.

7. Ibid., p. 431. That Mosley's membership in the war generation determined his political thought and action, and even the organizational forms he and his followers preferred, is clear. Ibid., pp. 49, 61, 70, 90-91, 100, 172-73, 229, 307, 340, 378, 382-83, 401-2, 414; Oswald Mosley, letter to *Books and Bookmen* 20 (July 1975):4. Mosley's generational consciousness led Winston Churchill to imprison him in May, 1940. Churchill had long before explicitly acknowledged the tension between him and the war generation. Winston S. Churchill, *The World Crisis 1911-1918*, vol. I (London: Odhams Press Limited, no date), p. ix.

8. Edwin Erich Dwinger, "The First Civil War in the West," in Panichas, ed., *Promise of Greatness*, pp. 217-25; Charles Petrie, "Fighting the First World War in London," in Panichas, ed., *Promise of Greatness*, p. 269; Sigmund Neumann, "The International Civil War," *World Politics* 1 (April 1949):333-50.

9. Richard Aldington, *Death of a Hero* (London: Chatto & Windus, 1929), p. 292; Charles Edmund Carrington, "Some Soldiers," in Panichas, ed., *Promise of Greatness*, p. 164; Lord Chandos, in *The Listener*, July 15, 1971, p. 74; Mildred Davidson, *The Poetry Is in the Pity* (New York: Barnes & Noble Books, 1972), p. 18; Sholto Douglas, *Years of Combat* (London: Collins, 1963), p. 201; Christopher Haworth, *March to Armistice 1918* (London: William Kimber, 1968), p. 26; Thomas Jones, *A Diary with Letters 1931-1950* (London: Oxford University Press, 1954), p. 250; Arthur E. Lane, *An Adequate Response: The War Poetry of Wilfred Owen & Siegfried Sassoon* (Detroit: Wayne State University Press, 1972), p. 25; Kingsley Martin, *Father Figures: A First Volume of Autobiography 1897-1931* (Hamondsworth, Eng.: Penguin Books, 1969), p. 80; Herbert Read, *The Contrary Experience: autobiographies* (London: Faber and Faber, 1963), p. 213; Herbert Read, Foreword to Panichas, ed., *Promise of Greatness*, p. v; Alan Thomas, *A Life Apart* (London: Victor Gollancz Ltd., 1968), p. 158; P. W. Turner and R. H. Haigh, *Not for Glory* (London: Robert Maxwell, 1969), p. 56; Alec Waugh, "A Light Rain Falling," in Panichas, ed., *Promise of Greatness*, p. 339; Henry Williamson, *The Pathway* (London: Faber and Faber, 1969), pp. 95, 227.

10. Daniel Horn, ed., *War, Mutiny and Revolution in the German Navy: The World War I Diary of Seaman Richard Stumpf* (New Brunswick, N. J.: Rutgers University Press, 1967), pp. 102, 109, 158, 242, 260; Martin Middlebrook, *The First Day on the Somme: 1 July 1916* (Glasgow: Fontana/

Collins, 1975), pp. 185, 233; James Stuart, *Within the Fringe: An Auto-biography* (London: The Bodley Head, 1967), p. 14; Lieut.-General Sir Brian Horrocks, *A Full Life* (London: Collins, 1961), pp. 18-20; Basil Willey, "A Schoolboy in the War," in Panichas, ed., *Promise of Greatness*, p. 329; Basil Willey, *Spots of Time: A Retrospect of the Years 1897-1920* (London: Chatto & Windus, 1965), pp. 215-16; Williamson, *The Golden Virgin*, p. 230; Guy Sajer, *The Forgotten Soldier*, trans. Lily Emmet (New York: Harper & Row, 1971), p. 144; Konstantin Paustovsky, *The Story of a Life*, trans. Joseph Barnes (New York: Pantheon Books, 1964), p. 289; Henry Williamson, *The Phoenix Generation* (London: Macdonald, 1965), p. 140; Graham H. Greenwell, *An Infant in Arms: War Letters of a Company Officer 1914-1918* (London: Allen Lane, The Penguin Press, 1972), pp. 136, 247-48. The same was true of civilians interned as prisoners. J. Davidson Ketchum, *Ruhleben: A Prison Camp Society* (Toronto: University of Toronto Press, 1965), pp. 84, 177. For more on the impact of Ruhleben, where allied civilians were prisoners of war, see T. H. Marshall, "A British sociological career," *International Social Science Journal* 25 (1973):89-90. For more on the immediate experience of being a civilian prisoner of war, see the ten numbers of *In Ruhleben Camp* (1915) and the five numbers of *The Ruhleben Camp Magazine* (1916), both published by such prisoners.

11. Haworth, *March to Armistice*, p. 115; Henry Williamson, *The Patriot's Progress* (London: Macdonald, 1968), p. 93.

12. Middlebrook, *The First Day on the Somme*, p. 59.

13. Ibid., p. 302.

14. H. Essame, *The Battle for Europe 1918* (London: B. T. Batsford, 1972), p. 11; Haworth, *March to Armistice*, pp. 61-62, 113; Turner and Haigh, *Not for Glory*, p. 66; Reginald Pound, *The Lost Generation of 1914* (New York: Coward-McCann, 1965), p. 234; Emilio Lussu, *Sardinian Brigade*, trans. Marion Rawson (Harrisburg, Pa.: Stackpole Books, 1967), p. 130; Stuart, *Within the Fringe*, p. 8; Eileen Quelch, *Perfect Darling: The Life and Times of George Cornwallis-West* (London: Cecil & Emelia Woolf, 1972), p. 122; Williamson, *The Golden Virgin*, p. 292, 295, 334; Henry Williamson, *Love and the Loveless: A Soldier's Tale* (London: Macdonald, 1958), pp. 136, 319; Williamson, *The Patriot's Progress*, pp. 180, 183; Greenwell, *An Infant in Arms*, p. 114; Middlebrook, *The First Day on the Somme*, pp. 234-35, 237, 247.

15. Middlebrook, *The First Day on the Somme*, p. 211.

16. Ibid., photograph opposite p. 239.

17. Mosley, *My Life*, pp. 60, 110; Williamson, *The Phoenix Generation*, p. 74; Williamson, *Love and the Loveless*, pp. 86, 120; Williamson, *The Pathway*, pp. 69-70, 110, 226; Pound, *The Lost Generation*, p. 177; Doug-

las, *Years of Combat*, pp. 149, 199-200, 233, 305; Haworth, *March to Armistice*, pp. 113-14, 127; Paolo Monelli, "Alpine Warfare," in Panichas, ed., *Promise of Greatness*, p. 130; Vladimir S. Littauer, *Russian Hussar* (London: J. A. Allen & Co. Ltd., 1965), pp. 240-41. This continued to be the case long after 1918. Sholto Douglas and Robert Wright, *Years of Command* (London: Collins, 1966), pp. 154-55, 330, 344, 346; see also Mosley, *My Life*, pp. 374-75.

18. Lewis, ed., *The Collected Poems of Wilfred Owen*, p. 82.

19. Adolf Hitler, *Mein Kampf*, trans. Ralph Manheim (Boston: Houghton Mifflin Company, 1943), p. 145.

20. Middlebrook, *The First Day on the Somme*, pp. 104, 213; Lord Moran, *The Anatomy of Courage* (Boston: Houghton Mifflin Company, 1967), pp. 50, 52, 55-56, 58; Pound, *The Lost Generation*, p. 158; Arthur Graeme West, *The Diary of a Dead Officer* (London: George Allen & Unwin Ltd., no date), pp. 12-13; C. M. Bowra, *Memories 1898-1939* (London: Weidenfeld and Nicolson, 1966), p. 90; Henry Williamson, *How Dear Is Life* (London: Macdonald, 1966), pp. 272, 279, 333; Williamson, *The Golden Virgin*, pp. 258, 296; Williamson, *Love and the Loveless*, pp. 154, 328.

21. Edmund Blunden, *Undertones of War* (London: Richard Cobden-Sanderson, 1928), pp. 214-15.

22. E. A. Mackintosh, "Recruiting," in *Up the Line to Death: The War Poets 1914-1918*, ed. Brian Gardner (London: Methuen & Co., Ltd., 1966), p. 111.

23. Ivor Gurney, "The Target," in Bernard Bergonzi, *Heroes' Twilight: A Study of the Great War* (London: Constable, 1965), p. 89.

24. Lewis, ed., *The Collected Poems of Wilfred Owen*, p. 36.

25. David Jones, *In Parenthesis* (New York: The Viking Press, 1963), p. xvii.

26. Lewis, ed., *The Collected Poems of Wilfred Owen*, p. 113.

27. Pound, *The Lost Generation*, p. 154.

28. Gerald Brenan, "A Survivor's Story," in Panichas, ed., *Promise of Greatness*, p. 41; Georges Gaudy, "Our Old Front," in Panichas, ed., *Promise of Greatness*, p. 90; Read, *The Contrary Experience*, p. 102; Henry Williamson, *The Dream of Fair Women* (London: Faber and Faber, 1968), p. 296.

29. Middlebrook, *The First Day on the Somme*, pp. 32, 59.

30. Ibid., p. 51.

31. Edward Thompson, *These Men Thy Friends* (London: Alfred A. Knopf, 1928), p. 120; Williamson, *Love and the Loveless*, p. 143; Greenwell, *An Infant in Arms*, p. 206; B. H. Liddell Hart, *History of the First World*

War (London: Pan Books Ltd., 1972), p. 464; Middlebrook, *The First Day on the Somme*, p. 203.

32. Douglas, *Years of Combat*, p. 234.

33. Greenwell, *An Infant in Arms*, pp. 113, 116; Williamson, *Love and the Loveless*, p. 143; Thompson, *These Men Thy Friends*, pp. 183, 198; Haworth, *March to Armistice*, p. 106; Montgomery Belgion, "A Reminiscence and a Meditation," in Panichas, ed., *Promise of Greatness*, p. 305; Monelli, "Alpine Warfare," p. 122; Naegelen, "Recollections," p. 178; Heinz H. E. Justus, "An Unconducted Tour of England," in *Escapers All* (London: The Bodley Head Ltd., 1934), p. 214; Horn, ed., *War, Mutiny and Revolution in the German Navy*, pp. 104, 156-57; Williamson, *The Phoenix Generation*, p. 355; Brigadier C. E. Lucas Phillips in *The Listener*, July 15, 1971, p. 74; Private 19022 [Frederick Manning], *Her Privates We* (London: Peter Davies, 1930), p. 14.

34. Carrington, "Some Soldiers," p. 165; Turner and Haigh, *Not for Glory*, p. 86; Littauer, *Russian Hussar*, p. 201.

35. Read, *The Contrary Experience*, p. 102; Williamson, *Love and the Loveless*, p. 12; Williamson, *The Dream of Fair Women*, pp. 216, 232; Manning, *Her Privates We*, p. 275; Vladimir Mayakovsky, *The Bedbug and Selected Poetry*, ed. Patricia Blake and trans. Max Hayward and George Reavey (New York: The World Publishing Company, 1970), pp. 117-19; Alfred F. Havighurst, *Twentieth-Century Britain*, 2nd ed. (New York: Harper & Row, 1966), p. 154.

36. Read, *The Contrary Experience*, p. 128; Williamson, *The Golden Virgin*, p. 229.

37. Naegelen, "Recollections," pp. 170-71.

38. Erich Maria Remarque, *All Quiet on the Western Front* (New York: Crest Books, 1964), p. 118; see also ibid., pp. 117, 119. There may have been some justification for this conclusion. Littauer, *Russian Hussar*, pp. 125-26.

39. Horn, ed., *War, Mutiny and Revolution in the German Navy*, p. 330.

40. West, *The Diary of a Dead Officer*, p. 80; see also Williamson, *Love and the Loveless*, p. 265; R. F. Delderfield, *To Serve Them All My Days* (New York: Simon and Schuster, 1972), pp. 35, 492.

41. Bergonzi, *Heroes' Twilight*, p. 53. For a different version of Sorley's letter, see Jon Silkin, *Out of Battle: The Poetry of the Great War* (London: Oxford University Press, 1972), p. 75.

42. Lewis, ed., *The Collected Poems of Wilfred Owen*, pp. 174-75; see also Harold Owen and John Bell, eds., *Wilfred Owen: Collected Letters* (London: Oxford University Press, 1967), p. 568; *Old Men Forget: The*

Autobiography of Duff Cooper (Viscount Norwich) (London: Rupert Hart-Davis, 1957), p. 194; Williamson, *The Phoenix Generation*, p. 175.

43. Middlebrook, *The First Day on the Somme*, p. 300.

44. L. Jessop, quoted in ibid., pp. 300-301.

45. Paustovsky, *The Story of a Life*, p. 314; see also ibid., p. 409.

46. Stuart Cloete, *How Young they Died* (London: Collins, 1969), p. 154; see also Littauer, *Russian Hussar*, pp. 178-79; Williamson, *The Pathway*, pp. 225-28; Robert Graves in *The Listener*, July 15, 1971, p. 74; Essame, *The Battle for Europe 1918*, p. 39; Mervyn Jones, *Holding On* (London: Quartet Books, 1973), p. 72; Middlebrook, *The First Day on the Somme*, pp. 299, 316.

47. Paustovsky, *The Story of a Life*, p. 387.

48. Cloete, *How Young they Died*, p. 91.

49. Greenwell, *An Infant in Arms*, p. 66.

50. Charles Edmonds [Charles Carrington], *A Subaltern's War* (London: Icon Books Limited, 1964), p. 16.

51. Erich Maria Remarque, *The Road Back*, trans. A. W. Wheen (New York: Avon Books, 1959), p. 91; see also Hannah Arendt, *The Origins of Totalitarianism* (New York: Meridian Books, 1958), pp. 329-30.

52. Graham Wootton, *The Politics of Influence: British ex-servicemen, Cabinet decisions and cultural change (1917-57)* (London: Routledge and Kegan Paul Ltd., 1965), pp. 71-72, 119, 262-63.

53. Ronald Tree, *When the Moon was High: Memoirs of Peace and War 1897-1942* (London: Macmillan & Co. Ltd., 1975), p. 64.

54. John P. Mackintosh, *The British Cabinet*, 2nd ed. (London: Methuen & Co. Ltd., 1968), p. 423.

55. J. A. Thompson and Arthur Mejia, Jr., *The Modern British Monarchy* (New York: St. Martin's Press, 1971), p. 77.

56. Remarque, *The Road Back*, p. 163; see also The Earl of Swinton, *Sixty Years of Power: Some memories of the men who wielded it* (London: Hutchinson, 1966), p. 144.

57. Hugh Dalton, *Towards the Peace of Nations: A Study in International Politics* (London: George Routledge & Sons, Ltd., 1928), pp. ix, 3-4; Douglas, *Years of Combat*, p. 43; Arthur Marwick, *The Deluge: British Society and the First World War* (Harmondsworth, Eng.: Penguin Books, 1967), p. 313; *Old Men Forget*, pp. 25, 49; Priestley, *Margin Released*, pp. 90, 102, 125, 186; Sir John Smyth, *The Only Enemy: An Autobiography* (London: Hutchinson, 1959), pp. 34, 44; Brigadier The Rt. Hon. Sir John Smyth, *Bolo Whistler: The Life of General Sir Lashmer Whistler GCB, KBE, DSO, DL: A Study in Leadership* (London: Frederick Muller, 1967), p. 34; Osbert Sitwell, *Great Morning* (London: Macmillan & Co. Ltd.,

1948), pp. 9, 229, 258-62, 265, 297; Mosley, *My Life*, p. 50; Williamson, *The Dream of Fair Women*, pp. 32, 87.

58. Lewis, ed., *The Collected Poems of Wilfred Owen*, p. 35. Ten million military deaths seems a minimal estimate. C. R. M. F. Cruttwell, *A History of the Great War 1914-1918* (Oxford: at the Clarendon Press, 1934), pp. 630-32; Gil Elliot, *Twentieth Century Book of the Dead* (London: Allen Lane Penguin Press, 1972), pp. 212, 215, 218.

59. Bentley B. Gilbert, *Britain Since 1918* (London: B. T. Batsford Ltd., 1967), p. 14; Turner and Haigh, *Not for Glory*, pp. 106-7; Smyth, *The Only Enemy*, p. 85; Sitwell, *Great Morning*, p. 229; Mosley, *My Life*, pp. 70, 378.

60. J. B. Priestley, *Margin Released: A Writer's Reminiscences and Reflections* (London: Heinemann, 1962), p. 121.

61. Eric Hiscock, *The Bells of Hell Go Ting-A-Ling-A-Ling: An Autobiographical Fragment without Maps* (London: Arlington Books, 1976), p. 82.

62. P. Smith, quoted by Middlebrook, *The First Day on the Somme*, p. 316.

63. Gilbert, *Britain Since 1918*, p. 11. On one day, July 1, 1916, British casualties approached sixty thousand men, the heaviest day's loss in British military history. Hiscock, *The Bells of Hell*, p. 118; Stuart, *Within the Fringe*, p. 16; *The Memoirs of Captain Liddell Hart*, vol. I (London: Cassell, 1967), p. 23; Churchill, *The World Crisis 1911-1918*, vol. II, p. 1077. Half of those British troops in the attack that day became casualties. Middlebrook, *The First Day on the Somme*, p. 263. Those casualties exceeded total British casualties in the Crimean War, the Boer War, and the Korean War combined. Ibid., p. 265. The Somme was literally "the abattoir" of the war generation. Robert Penn Warren, *A Place to Come To* (New York: Random House, 1977), p. 69. By November 14, 1916, British troops had advanced exactly six miles, and total casualties on the Somme were over 1,300,000, divided almost equally between German and Allied troops. Middlebrook, *The First Day on the Somme*, p. 295. Even more may have been lost than one generation: "From the watershed of the Somme, from charred wood and desolated valley, amidst the fragmentation of steel and flesh and the dust of detonated village hanging in the sun, was coming the thought that would bring not only the end of the old order, but the end of ideas that had endured a thousand years." Williamson, *The Golden Virgin*, p. 340.

64. Walter Z. Laqueur, *Young Germany: A History of the German Youth Movement* (New York: Basic Books, 1962), p. 97.

65. Hitler, *Mein Kampf*, p. 335.

66. Frank Owen, *Tempestuous Journey: Lloyd George: His Life and times* (London: Hutchinson, 1954), p. 522.

67. Charles P. Kindleberger, *Economic Growth in France and Britain 1851-1950* (Cambridge: Harvard University Press, 1967), p. 79. Total French casualties approximated 5,651,000. Lane, *An Adequate Response*, p. 37.

68. Herbert Luethy, *France Against Herself*, trans. Eric Mosbacher (New York: Meridian Books, 1958), p. 78.

69. *Editorial: The Memoirs of Colin R. Coote* (London: Eyre & Spottis-woode, 1965), p. 36. The fear of another Somme or another Verdun was not confined to France. This fear made British military leaders "in the Second World War, most of whom had served as young men in the earlier war, so determined to find the right answers to stalemate and attrition," Douglas, *Years of Combat*, p. 153; see also General Sir Richard Gale, *Call to Arms: An Autobiography* (London: Hutchinson, 1968), p. 54. This fear was also the basis for the strategic thinking of the most gifted military mind within the war generation, whose entire career after 1918 was devoted "to ensure that if war came again there should be no repetition of the Somme and Passchendaele." *The Memoirs of Captain Liddell Hart*, vol. II (London: Cassell, 1965), p. 101. During World War II, Liddell Hart favored a negotiated peace settlement. Paul Addison, "Lloyd George and Compromise Peace in the Second World War," in *Lloyd George: Twelve Essays*, ed. A. J. P. Taylor (New York: Atheneum, 1971), p. 377. July 1, 1916, clearly left a lasting impression on Liddell Hart. Middlebrook, *The First Day on the Somme*, p. 238. Ironically, the great air battles between Britain and Germany in 1940 were commanded on both sides by senior officers who had first faced each other as young pilots in World War I. Douglas and Wright, *Years of Command*, pp. 28, 30, 99.

70. *Four Plays by Sophocles*, trans. Theodore Howard Banks (New York: Oxford University Press, 1966), p. 132. For a contradiction to Sophocles, see Paavo Rintala, *Nahkapeitturien linjalla I: Romaani* (Helsinki: Kustannusosakeyhtiö Otava, 1976), p. 209.

71. Patrick MacGill, *Soldier Songs* (New York: E. P. Dutton & Co., 1917), p. 91; see also Lieut.-General Sir Frederick Morgan, *Peace and War: A Soldier's Life* (London: Hodder and Stoughton, 1961), p. 312.

72. Moran, *The Anatomy of Courage*, pp. 108, 110; Pound, *The Lost Generation*, p. 259; *Old Men Forget*, p. 32.

73. *Old Men Forget*, p. 261;; see also E. Thornton Cook, *What Manner of Men? Our Prime Ministers in Action and Word from J. Ramsay Macdonald to Benjamin Disraeli (Lord Beaconsfield)* (London: Heath Cranton Limited, 1934), p. 63.

74. Pound, *The Lost Generation*, pp. 153, 319, 226, 273; Harold Macmillan, *Winds of Change 1914-1939* (New York: Harper & Row, 1966), p. 78; Read, *The Contrary Experience*, p. 61.

75. *The Early Years of Alec Waugh* (New York: Farrar, Straus and Company, 1963), pp. 92, 138; Gilbert, *Britain Since 1918*, p. 14; Marwick, *The Deluge*, pp. 335-36; J. B. Priestley, *The Edwardians* (New York: Harper & Row, 1970), p. 289; Malcolm Thomson, *Churchill: His Life and Times* (London: Odhams Books Limited, 1965), p. 170; Lord Robbins, *Autobiography of an Economist* (London: Macmillan & Co. Ltd., 1971), p. 47; Malcolm Thomson, *David Lloyd George: The Official Biography* (London: Hutchinson, no date), p. 257.

76. Robert Rhodes James, *Churchill: A Study in Failure 1900-1939* (Harmondsworth, Eng.: Penguin Books, 1973), p. 129; Max Beloff, *Imperial Sunset: Volume I: Britain's Liberal Empire, 1897-1921* (New York: Alfred A. Knopf, 1970), p. 247.

77. Robert Graves, *Goodbye to All That*, rev. ed. (Garden City, N.Y.: Doubleday & Company, 1957), p. 59; see also Delderfield, *To Serve Them All My Days*, p. 21; Graham Greene, *A Sort of Life* (New York: Pocket Books, 1973), p. 76.

78. Sir John Slessor, *These Remain: A Personal Anthology* (London: Michael Joseph, 1969), p. 21.

79. Macmillan, *Winds of Change*, p. 45; Anthony Sampson, *Macmillan: A Study in Ambiguity* (London: Allen Lane, The Penguin Press, 1967), p. 13.

80. Sir Ernest Barker, *Age and Youth: Memories of Three Universities and Father of the Man* (London: Oxford University Press, 1953), p. 77; see also Hiscock, *The Bells of Hell*, p. 141; Sir Charles Petrie, *A Historian Looks at His World* (London: Sidgwick & Jackson, 1972), p. 51.

81. Smyth, *Bolo Whistler*, p. 37.

82. Turner and Haigh, *Not for Glory*, p. 101; Arthur Marwick, *Britain in the Century of Total War: War, Peace and Social Change 1900-1967* (Harmondsworth, Eng.: Penguin Books, 1970), p. 62; Beloff, *Imperial Sunset*, vol. I, p. 278.

83. Blythe, *Akenfield*, p. 44.

84. *Churchill: Taken from the Diaries of Lord Moran: The Struggle for Survival 1940-1965* (Boston: Houghton Mifflin Company, 1966), p. 321.

85. MacGill, *Soldier Songs*, p. 23.

86. Robert Nichols, *Ardours and Endurances* (London: Chatto & Windus, 1917), p. 56.

87. Aldington, *Death of a Hero*, p. 227; Lewis, ed., *The Collected Poems of Wilfred Owen*, p. 77; Remarque, *The Road Back*, pp. 162-63; Williamson, *How Dear is Life*, pp. 278-79.

88. Priestley, *Margin Released*, p. 136; see also Williamson, *Love and the Loveless*, p. 166; S. E. Cryer, letter to *Daily Express*, December 1, 1976, p. 14.

89. *The Iliad*, trans. Alston Hurd Chase and William G. Perry, Jr. (No place: Little, Brown and Company, 1950), p. 439.

90. Laqueur, *Young Germany*, p. 90.

91. *Old Men Forget*, p. 69.

92. Ernst Jünger, *On the Marble Cliffs*, trans. Stuart Hood (Harmondsworth, Eng.: Penguin Books, 1970), p. 77; *The Poems of Edmund Blunden 1914-30* (London: Cobden-Sanderson, 1930), p. 50.

93. Remarque, *All Quiet*, p. 77; Williamson, *The Pathway*, p. 289; Williamson, *The Dream of Fair Women*, pp. 44-45, 202, 440.

94. Remarque, *The Road Back*, p. 160.

95. Ibid., p. 190.

96. Remarque, *All Quiet*, p. 174.

97. Anthony Powell, *At Lady Molly's* (New York: Popular Library, 1976), p. 21.

98. Remarque, *All Quiet*, p. 56.

99. Lewis, ed., *The Collected Poems of Wilfred Owen*, p. 69.

100. A model along these lines is the poem "On the Poor B. B.," in Bertolt Brecht, *Manual of Piety*, trans. Eric Bentley (New York: Grove Press, 1966), p. 249.

101. C. M. Bowra, *Poetry & Politics 1900-1960* (Cambridge: at the University Press, 1965), p. 120; Martin Esslin, *Brecht: The Man and His Work* (Garden City, N. Y.: Doubleday & Company, 1961), p. 7; Bowra, *Memories*, pp. 116, 123; Douglas, *Years of Combat*, p. 340; Edmonds, *A Subaltern's War*, p. 11; Morgan, *Peace and War*, pp. 42, 59-60; Turner and Haigh, *Not for Glory*, p. xiii; Ernest Parker, *Into Battle 1914-1918* (London: Longmans, Green and Co., 1964), p. 20.

102. Aldington, *Death of a Hero*, p. 32.

103. Ibid., p. 377.

104. *The Poems of Edmund Blunden*, pp. 163, 166, 170.

105. Ibid., p. 171.

106. Herbert, *The Secret Battle*, p. 166: Douglas, *Years of Combat*, pp. 340-41, 346; Douglas and Wright, *Years of Command*, p. 13; Havighurst, *Twentieth-Century Britain*, p. 155.

107. Hector Bolitho, *A Century of British Monarchy* (London: Longmans, Green and Co., 1951), p. 195; *A King's Story: The Memoirs of the Duke of Windsor* (New York: G. P. Putnam's Sons, 1951), pp. 119, 127, 132; Pierre Berton, *The Royal Family: The Story of the British Monarchy from Victoria to Elizabeth* (New York: Alfred A. Knopf, 1954), pp. 111-12; Sir Charles

Petrie, *The Modern British Monarchy* (London: Eyre & Spottiswoode, 1961), p. 163; Charles Loch Mowat, *Britain Between the Wars 1918-1940* (London: Methuen & Co. Ltd., 1968), p. 582; Williamson, *The Phoenix Generation*, p. 247; Ursula Bloom, *The Duke of Windsor* (London: Robert Hale, 1972), pp. 46, 93, 123; Thompson and Mejia, *The Modern British Monarchy*, p. 72.

108. Aldington, *Death of a Hero*, pp. 333-34.

109. George Coppard, *With a machine gun to Cambrai* (London: Her Majesty's Stationery Office, 1969), p. 133; Richard Aldington, *Life for Life's Sake: A Book of Reminiscences* (London: Cassell, 1968), p. 188; *The Last Englishman: an autobiography of Lieut.-Col. Alfred Daniel Wintle M. C. (1st the Royal Dragoons)* (London: Michael Joseph, 1968), pp. 45-46; Martin, *Father Figures*, pp. 86-87; Williamson, *The Phoenix Generation*, p. 48; Mosley, *My Life*, Preface to the American Edition and p. 73.

110. C. A. Turner, quoted in Middlebrook, *The First Day on the Somme*, p. 309.

111. Priestley, *Margin Released*, p. 88; see also Powell, *At Lady Molly's*, p. 178.

112. Delderfield, *To Serve Them All My Days*, p. 14.

113. *The Poems of Edmund Blunden*, p. 45.

114. Desmond Young, *Rommel* (London: Collins, 1950), p. 50.

115. Paul Fussell, *The Great War and Modern Memory* (New York: Oxford University Press, 1975), p. 74.

116. Jones, *Holding On*, p. 70.

117. Marwick, *The Deluge*, pp. 335-36; Sitwell, *Great Morning*, pp. 260, 268.

118. Mowat, *Britain Between the Wars*, p. 9.

119. Ibid., p. 6; see also Bernard Barker, ed., *Ramsay MacDonald's Political Writings* (London: Allen Lane, The Penguin Press, 1972), p. 4. That result must have unpleasantly surprised the chief Coalition Liberal whip, who wrote to Lloyd George in July 1918: "With reference to the 'khaki' voters, especially abroad, could not something be done to ensure their vote being cast for the government?" Trevor Wilson, "The Coupon and the British General Election of 1918," *The Journal of Modern History* 36 (March 1964):35.

120. Wootton, *The Politics of Influence*, p. 205n.

121. Gardner, ed., *Up the Line to Death*, p. 107. This song was an adaptation of an earlier song with another message. John Brophy and Eric Partridge, *The Long Trail: What the British Soldier Sang and Said in the Great War of 1914-18* (New York: London House & Maxwell, 1965), p. 70. Or was it another message?

122. Macmillan, *Winds of Change*, p. 98.

123. Charles Carrington, *Soldier from the Wars Returning* (New York: David McKay Company, 1965), p. 243; Graves, *Goodbye to All That*, pp. 287, 293; Thompson, *These Men Thy Friends*, pp. 214-15; A. R. Cooper, *March or Bust: Adventures in the Foreign Legion* (London: Robert Hale & Company, 1972), pp. 203-4.

124. Barker, *Age and Youth*, p. 83.

125. Bowra, *Memories*, p. 97.

126. Jünger, *On the Marble Cliffs*, p. 54.

127. Read, *The Contrary Experience*, p. 124.

128. Ibid., p. 128. This brief diary entry is the necessary background for understanding Herbert Read, *Anarchy and Order: Essays in Politics* (Boston: Beacon Press, 1971). See also W. H. Lewis, ed., *Letters of C. S. Lewis* (New York: Harcourt Brace Jovanovich, 1975), p. 281.

129. Aldington, *Death of a Hero*, p. 17; see also Thompson, *These Men Thy Friends*, pp. 284-85.

130. Read, *The Contrary Experience*, p. 60; see also Sir Dingle Foot, *British Political Crises* (London: William Kimber, 1976), pp. 125-26.

131. Read, *The Contrary Experience*, p. 65; see also Martin, *Father Figures*, p. 99.

132. Read, *The Contrary Experience*, pp. 217-18.

133. "The part played by the bourgeoisie is finished— permanently, my party comrades," said Hitler in 1932. Hermann Rauschning, *Hitler Speaks: A Series of Political Conversations with Adolf Hitler on his Real Aims* (London: Thornton Butterworth Ltd., 1939), pp. 48-49.

134. Hitler, *Mein Kampf*, p. 491.

135. Ibid., p. 246.

136. Ibid., pp. 175, 206; Edouard Calic, *Unmasked: Two Confidential Interviews with Hitler in 1931*, trans. Richard Barry (London: Chatto & Windus, 1971), pp. 48, 85; Mosley, *My Life*, p. 70. Politics was, of course, not the only vocation discovered in the war. Charles Petrie, "Fighting the First World War in London," p. 262; Petrie, *A Historian Looks at His World*, pp. 37-38. It was even possible to discover that politics was almost, but not quite, one's vocation. Jean Lacouture, *De Gaulle*, trans. Francis K. Price (New York: Avon Books, 1968), p. 28; Marshall, "A British Sociological Career," p. 90.

137. Wm. K. Pfeiler, *War and the German Mind: The Testimony of Men of Fiction Who Fought at the Front* (New York: AMS Press, 1966), p. 48. "I don't say I regretted the coming of the second war in any way at all." Brigadier C. E. Lucas Phillips, in *The Listener*, July 15, 1971, p. 75.

138. Hans Rogger, "Afterthoughts," in *The European Right: A Historical*

Profile, ed. Hans Rogger and Eugen Weber (Berkeley: University of California Press, 1965), pp. 586-87.

139. Sigmund Neumann, "The Conflict of Generations in Contemporary Europe: From Versailles to Munich," *Vital Speeches of the Day* 5 (August 1, 1939):625.

140. Hitler, *Mein Kampf*, p. 198; see also Werner and Lotte Pelz, *I am Adolf Hitler* (London: SCM Press, 1969), p. 89.

141. Hitler, *Mein Kampf*, p. 161; see also Pelz and Pelz, *I am Adolf Hitler*, pp. 84-85.

142. Hitler, *Mein Kampf*, pp. 163-64.

143. August Kubizek, *Young Hitler: The Story of Our Friendship*, trans. E. V. Anderson (London: Allan Wingate, 1954), p. 118.

144. Franz Jetzinger, *Hitler's Youth*, trans. Lawrence Wilson (London: Hutchinson, 1958); Bradley F. Smith, *Adolf Hitler: His Family, Childhood and Youth* (Stanford, Calif.: The Hoover Institution, 1967); Marvin Rintala, "The Death of Nietzsche and the Birth of Hitler," *The Review of Politics* 31 (January 1969):124-29.

145. Pfeiler, *War and the German Mind*, p. 5.

146. Francis Foster, "Holy Ground," in Panichas, ed., *Promise of Greatness*, p. 318; Brigadier C. E. Lucas Phillips, in *The Listener*, July 15, 1971, pp. 74-75; Mosley, *My Life*, p. 69.

147. Greenwell, *An Infant in Arms*, p. 41.

148. Bettina L. Knapp, *Antonin Artaud: Man of Vision* (New York: Avon Books, 1971).

149. Paul Piazza, "A Literary Cartographer of Conviction," *The Chronicle of Higher Education*, May 1, 1978, p. 15.

150. Arne Somersalo, *Taisteluvuosien varrelta: suomalaisen sotilaan muistelmia maailmansodasta* (Helsinki: Kustannusosakeyhtiö Otava, 1928), pp. 10-11; see Pelz and Pelz, *I am Adolf Hitler*, pp. 158-61.

151. Bradley F. Smith, *Heinrich Himmler: A Nazi in the Making, 1900-1926* (Stanford, Calif.: Hoover Institution Press, 1971), pp. 66, 93, 132, 134; Mosley, *My Life*, pp. 303-4.

152. Charles de Gaulle, *France and Her Army*, trans. F. L. Dash (London: Hutchinson, no date), p. 71. "The First War turned me unexpectedly into a 'sword man.' Action—harsh, brutal, compelling—ousted learning. The gown was exchanged for a tunic." Harold Macmillan, *Riding the Storm 1956-1959* (London: Macmillan & Co., Ltd., 1971), p. 197; see also Swinton, *Sixty Years of Power*, pp. 174-75.

153. Charles de Gaulle, *The Edge of the Sword*, trans. Gerard Hopkins (New York: Criterion Books, 1960), p. 9; see also Mosely, *My Life*, p. 136.

154. Pfeiler, *War and the German Mind*, p. 112.

155. Lord Boothby, "Mosley: a wasted potential," *Books and Bookmen* 20 (May 1975): 31.

156. Before 1940 one militant member of the war generation referred to "the court of War, that heartless, though by no means unjust judge." De Gaulle, *France and Her Army*, p. 90.

157. Rauschning, *Hitler Speaks*, pp. 46-47.

158. Erich Maria Remarque, *The Black Obelisk* (New York: Crest Books, 1957), p. 98. In late 1919, after joining a ready reserve unit of the *Reichswehr*, Heinrich Himmler wrote in his diary: "Today I have put the uniform on again. For me it is always the most precious clothing one can wear." Smith, *Heinrich Himmler*, p. 78. For the pacific members of the war generation, on the other hand: "However hard pressed, even desperate, I may have been at times in the years after the war, never for one moment did I long to be back in the Army." Priestley, *Margin Released*, p. 89.

159. Smith, *Heinrich Himmler*, p. 89.

160. *The Owl of Minerva: The Autobiography of Gustav Regler*, trans. Norman Denny (New York: Farrar, Straus and Cudahy, 1959), p. 73; see also Alden Hatch, *The de Gaulle Nobody Knows: An Intimate Biography of Charles de Gaulle* (New York: Hawthorn Books, 1960), p. 44; Cecil Roberts, *The Years of Promise: Being the Second Book of an Autobiography: 1908-1919* (London: Hodder and Stoughton, 1968), p. 70; *The last Englishman*, p. 106.

161. Gaudy, "Our Old Front," p. 95.

162. Foster, "Holy Ground," p. 320. The image of Gethsemane was also used of himself by a member of the war generation who went to prison rather than serve in the military. Lord Taylor of Mansfield, *Uphill All the Way: A Miner's Struggle* (London: Sidgwick & Jackson, 1972), pp. 27-28.

163. Blunden, *Undertones of War*, p. 148; Williamson, *The Golden Virgin*, p. 105; Williamson, *Love and the Loveless*, p. 120; Henry Williamson in *The Listener*, July 15, 1971, p. 73.

164. Cyril Falls, *War Books: A Critical Guide* (London: Peter Davies, 1930), p. x; Nichols, *Ardours*, pp. 6, 48.

165. Nichols, *Ardours*, p. 14.

166. Jones, *In Parenthesis*, p. x.

167. George Santayana, *The Last Puritan: A Memoir in the Form of a Novel* (New York: Charles Scribner's Sons, 1961), p. 523; Carrington, *Soldier from the Wars Returning*, p. 219; Macmillan, *Winds of Change*, p. 100; Nichols, *Ardours*, p. 12; Brenan, "A Survivor's Story," p. 46; *Old Men Forget*, p. 85; Ilse Ollendorff Reich, *Wilhelm Reich: A Personal Biography* (New York: Avon Books, 1970), pp. 26-27; Greenwell, *An Infant in Arms*, pp. xxi, 117, 147, 159, 168, 198-99, 251; Smyth, *The Only*

Enemy, p. 68; Ronald W. Clark, *JBS: The Life and Work of J. B. S. Haldane* (New York: Coward-McCann, 1969), pp. 35-37, 40, 48; Williamson, *How Dear Is Life*, pp. 245, 272, 298; Williamson, *The Golden Virgin*, p. 285; Williamson, *The Patriot's Progress*, pp. 66, 71.

168. "The Ole Sweats," in Macgill, *Soldier Songs*, p. 28.

169. "Letters," in ibid., p. 55. Such equality could be overstated, as is apparent in Wootton, *The Politics of Influence*, p. 83.

170. In the sense of Ferdinand Tönnies, *Fundamental Concepts of Sociology (Gemeinschaft und Gesellschaft)*, trans. and suppl. Charles P. Loomis (New York: American Book Company, 1940).

171. Aldington, *Life*, p. 96; Blunden, *Undertones of War*, pp. 178; 201, 224; Bowra, *Memories*, pp. 90-91; Coppard, *With a machine gun to Cambrai*, p. 107; Delderfield, *To Serve Them All My Days*, p. 165; Gardner, ed., *Up the Line to Death*, p. xxii; Haworth, *March to Armistice*, p. 54; Jones, *In Parenthesis*, pp. xxi, 37; Lewis, ed., *The Collected Poems of Wilfred Owen*, p. 39; Macmillan, *Winds of Change*, p. 99; *The Memoirs of Captain Liddell Hart*, vol. I, p. 17; Panichas, ed., *Promise of Greatness*, p. xxi; Vivian de Sola Pinto, "My First War: Memoirs of a Spectacled Subaltern," in Panichas, ed., *Promise of Greatness*, pp. 75, 78; Read, *The Contrary Experience*, pp. 66, 216; Read, Foreword to Panichas, ed., *Promise of Greatness*, p. vi; Herbert Read, "My Company," in Gardner, ed., *Up the Line to Death*, p. 87; Thompson, *These Men Thy Friends*, p. 284; Turner and Haigh, *Not for Glory*, p. 102; Clark, *JBS*, pp. 53-64; Pelz and Pelz, *I am Adolf Hitler*, p. 86; Williamson, *The Pathway*, pp. 70, 289; Williamson, *The Phoenix Generation*, pp. 307, 350.

172. Young, *Rommel*, p. 49; Mosely, *My Life*, p. 305; Wootton, *The Politics of Influence*, pp. 65, 219, 256.

173. Arthur J. Vidich and Maurice R. Stein, "The Dissolved Identity in Military Life," *Identity and Anxiety: Survival of the Person in Mass Society*, ed. Maurice R. Stein, Arthur J. Vidich, and David Manning White (Glencoe, Ill.: The Free Press, 1969), p. 503.

174. Remarque, *All Quiet*, p. 138.

175. *The Early Years of Alec Waugh*, p. 114; see also *Editorial*, p. 88; Kingsley Martin, *Editor: A Second Volume of Autobiography 1931-1945* (Harmondsworth, Eng.: Penguin Books, 1969), p. 13.

176. Haworth, *March to Armistice*, pp. 26, 54; Thomas, *A Life Apart*, p. 160; Lord Boothby, "From Geneva to Armageddon," *Books and Bookmen* 19 (July 1974):12.

177. Bowra, *Memories*, p. 94.

178. Charles Hamilton Sorley, *Marlborough and Other Poems* (Cambridge: at the University Press, 1922), p. 73.

179. Haworth, *March to Armistice*, p. 89.

180. Delderfield, *To Serve Them All My Days*, p. 106.

181. Wootton, *The Politics of Influence*, p. 87.

182. Haworth, *March to Armistice*, p. 171.

183. Lewis, ed., *The Collected Poems of Wilfred Owen*, p. 12.

184. Hans Kohn, *Living in a World Revolution: My Encounters with History* (New York: Simon and Schuster, 1970), p. 105; Martin, *Father Figures*, p. 102; Harold L. Poor, *Kurt Tucholsky and the Ordeal of Germany 1914-1935* (New York: Charles Scribner's Sons, 1968), p. 40; Penelope Gilliatt, "Master Movie-Maker," *Observer Review*, March 30, 1975, p. 17.

185. West, *The Diary of a Dead Officer*, p. 58.

186. Bergonzi, *Heroes' Twilight*, p. 109.

187. Willey, "A Schoolboy in the War," p. 331.

188. Waugh, "A Light Rain Falling," p. 343.

189. Paustovsky, *The Story of a Life*, p. 370.

190. F. W. A. Turner, quoted in Middlebrook, *The First Day on the Somme*, p. 310.

191. Lewis, ed., *The Collected Poems of Wilfred Owen*, p. 167; see also Owen and Bell, eds., *Wilfred Owen*, p. 461.

192. Horn, ed., *War, Mutiny and Revolution in the German Navy*, p. 398.

193. Gordon Bottomley and Denys Harding, eds., *The Collected Poems of Isaac Rosenberg* (New York: Schocken Books, 1949), p. 124; Raymond Postgate, "A Socialist Remembers—2," *New Statesman*, April 16, 1971, p. 526.

194. Laqueur, *Young Germany*, p. 89.

195. Paul Bewsher, "Nox Mortis," in Gardner, ed., *Up the Line to Death*, p. 56.

196. Lewis, ed., *The Collected Poems of Wilfred Owen*, p. 85.

197. Remarque, *The Road Back*, p. 51.

198. R. K. Sheridan, *Kurt von Schuschnigg: A Tribute* (London: The English Universities Press Ltd., 1942), p. 22.

199. P. H. B. Lyon, "Now to be Still and Rest," in Gardner, ed., *Up the Line to Death*, p. 147.

200. Aldous Huxley, *Antic Hay* (New York: Harper & Row, 1965), p. 14.

201. Martin, *Father Figures*, p. 111; Martin, *Editor*, pp. 42, 184; Sampson, *Macmillan*, p. 226; Wootton, *The Politics of Influence*, p. 270.

202. Francis Williams in Mervyn Jones, ed., *Kingsley Martin: Portrait and Self-portrait* (London: Barrie & Jenkins, 1969), p. 71.

203. Erich Maria Remarque, *Three Comrades*, trans. A. W. Wheen (New York: Popular Library, 1964), p. 49.

204. Karl Mannheim, "The Problem of Generations," in his *Essays on the Sociology of Knowledge*, ed. Paul Kecskemeti (London: Routledge and Kegan Paul Ltd., 1952), p. 283.

205. Ibid., pp. 304, 306-7.

206. Powell, *At Lady Molly's* p. 171; Gardner, ed., *Up the Line to Death*, p. xx; Herbert, *The Secret Battle*, p. 202; Delderfield, *To Serve Them All My Days* p. 37; Parker, *Into Battle*, p. 96; Christopher Sykes, *Evelyn Waugh: A Biography* (Boston: Little, Brown and Company, 1975), pp. 44-45; Roberts, *The Years of Promise*, pp. 267-68.

207. Panichas, Introduction to Panichas, ed., *Promise of Greatness*, p. xxii.

208. Carrington, "Some Soldiers," p. 157.

209. Mannheim, "The Problem of Generations," p. 314.

210. Osbert Sitwell, *Left Hand, Right Hand!* (London: Macmillan & Co. Ltd., 1952), p. 172.

211. Carrington, *Soldier From the Wars Returning*, p. 87.

212. Bergonzi, *Heroes' Twilight*, p. 120.

213. Remarque, *The Road Back*, p. 161.

214. Smith, *Still Quiet on the Western Front*, p. 91.

215. H. C. Bloor, quoted in Middlebrook, *The First Day on the Somme*, p. 314.

216. Willey, *Spots of Time*, p. 244.

217. Carrington, "Some Soldiers," p. 157.

218. Williamson, *The Dream of Fair Women*, p. 429.

Essay 3

Generational Conflict Within the Finnish Army

Because of the common lack of an organizational basis for the expression of generational differences, the conflict of generations commonly takes place within, rather than between or among, institutions. Generational conflict can, and often does, take place within a wide variety of institutional contexts, ranging from factories to universities, from parties to states. One institutional context in which generational conflict is both frequent and politically significant is that of armies. "In the army, as everywhere else, men of different generations have a hard time seeing eye to eye."[1] As the careers of Charles de Gaulle and Basil Liddell Hart suggest, members of the war generation were involved in generational conflict within a number of European armies after 1918. This conflict had important consequences for the armies as well as the individuals involved, and for Europe as a whole as well as individual nations. One army in which generational conflict was particularly bitter and particularly important after World War I was the Finnish Army. The case of the Finnish Army is especially instructive both for an understanding of generational differences within a specific institutional context and for an understanding of the determination with which the European war generation of 1914-18 acted to preserve the values acquired in its formative years.

When Finland became a Grand Duchy of the Russian Emperor in 1809, it was permitted to maintain a national army completely independent of the Russian Imperial Army. In 1901, however, as part of an intensive Russification effort, the Emperor abolished the

Finnish Army. The declaration of Finnish independence in December 1917 found Finland without an army. The creation of an effective national army was therefore one of the major immediate problems of an independent Finland. Whatever may have been the prospects of arms reduction among the established military powers, Finland was not in a position to assume anything else but that armed strength was necessary for continued independence. The Winter War of 1939-40 was to demonstrate with terrible clarity the appropriateness of this Finnish pessimism. The vigorous response of the Finnish Army to Soviet military power in that war demonstrated dramatically that an effective national army had been created. The difficulties encountered in this creation were many and important. Parliament consistently tended toward parsimony in appropriations for the national defense establishment.[2] Serious disagreement prevailed among the parties over the form and duration of conscription. The latest developments in military science and technology often made belated arrivals in Finland.

The military difficulty that assumed the greatest political significance during the first decade of independence was, however, none of these. The paramount difficulty was the creation of a trained and loyal corps of officers. When the Finnish Army was abolished in 1901, its officers entered other careers. The achievement of independence saw these former officers dead, retired, or permanently settled in new careers. The corps of Finnish officers during the first decade of independence therefore consisted virtually *in toto* of two distinct groups: Finnish-born *Jägers* in the German Army during World War I, and Finnish-born former career officers in the Russian Imperial Army. The latter were, for the most part, much older than the former *Jägers* and thus filled the posts of highest command in the new Finnish Army. They included[3] Karl Wilkama (formerly Wilkman), Ernst Löfström, Paul von Gerich, Oskar Enckell, and K. E. Berg, among many others. These two generations of Finnish officers were never reconciled to each other. The conflict between them after 1918 was the result of far more serious causes than divergent approaches to the art of war learned in German and Russian armies. These two generations of Finnish officers had fundamentally different world views, which can be understood only by comparing their formative experiences.

The roots of the former *Jägers* were in World War I, and they were clearly members of the European war generation of 1914-18. The beginning of that war came when the effort to Russify Finland was already fifteen years old. Although Finland remained free of World War I as far as direct military participation was concerned, the war intensified attempts by the Russian government to reduce the practical significance of Finnish autonomy. The increasing improbability of a development of the Russo-Finnish relationship favorable to the latter became apparent to a small group of young Finns, primarily university students and recent university graduates. They saw in a Russian military defeat the only opportunity to gain Finnish independence, or even to regain autonomy. These young Finns therefore joined an illegal movement, financially supported by Germany, intended to provide them with professional military training in the German Army, followed by active service against the Russian Imperial Army on the Eastern Front.

For the two thousand young Finns who shared in the experiences of the German Army during World War I, these years were decisive. They were organized upon their arrival in Germany into a *Jäger* battalion. "They became Prussian soldiers and they were drilled and treated as such."[4] The degree to which they accommodated themselves to a measure of discipline they had never before encountered surprised German officers.[5] That these future Finnish officers should accept a Prussian standard of discipline was perhaps understandable, since they knew the practices of no other army.[6] Their eagerness for actual participation in battle against Russian troops[7] was even more understandable. This eagerness was satisfied in 1916. The visible symbols of success became Iron Crosses and mention in Orders-of-the-Day.[8]

These years saw the alienation from politics—even that of their homeland—of the *Jäger* battalion members.[9] Isolated—partly for linguistic reasons—from news of the world at large, and knowing almost nothing of what was happening in Finland,[10] the *Jägers* developed an intense sense of comradeship during these years that made of the battalion a true community—*Gemeinschaft*—in the sense of Ferdinand Tönnies.[11] These shared experiences were the historical origin of that sense of comradeship-in-arms—in Finnish, *asevelihenki*—that bound the *Jägers* together throughout their political and physical lives, until 1941-44, when it achieved its culmination in a renewal of the German-Finnish *Waffenbrüder-schaft*.[12] Even though they had prepared themselves in the university for other, unrelated careers, many of the *Jäger* battalion members chose to become professional soldiers after 1918, forming the core of the Finnish officer corps before and during 1939-44.[13]

The *Jägers* found the meaning of their lives in total devotion to the Finnish nation, whose independence of Russia was literally their cause. Not only were they Finnish nationalists, but they were totally opposed to everything Russian. For them Russia was the mortal enemy of Finland. For them nothing good could come from Russia, especially from its army. They literally hated Russia.[14] Ironically, they found themselves commanded in and after 1918 by cosmopolite generals and colonels who had spent decades in the voluntary service of the Russian Emperor. It is important to recall that most of the three thousand Finns who sought and found careers as officers in Russia did so before 1901, while there was still a Finnish Army. Almost four hundred Finns rose to the rank of general or admiral in the Imperial Forces under the last four Romanov rulers.[15] These Finns felt quite at home. Between 1809 and 1899 the Russian Emperors generally acted with sagacity in their capacity as Grand Dukes of Finland. Throughout the Empire Finns had the rights of Russian subjects, although Russians did not get corresponding rights in Finland until 1912. Like most of the premodern armies, that of Imperial Russia was still prenationalist.[16] There was a strong sense of camaraderie in the multinational officer corps, and Russian chauvinism was notable by its absence, even at the breakfast table.[17]

These Finnish officers found in the Russian Imperial Army not only high ranks, but substantial social prestige. Many of them married Russian women;[18] Mannerheim and Löfström, for instance, married daughters of Russian generals. The grandeur of the final decades of the Russian Empire—many Finnish officers served in Asian Russia—impressed itself indelibly upon young officers accustomed to the relatively narrow confines of Finnish territory and society. They became fond of—and some were overwhelmed by—life on the grand scale of St. Petersburg. Stationed in Vladivostok, one of them wrote: "I miss St. Petersburg."[19] The most cosmopolitan of all Finnish soldiers expressed this reaction with his customary precision, recalling his departure from Russia in December 1917:

> My thirty years of service in the Imperial Army were ended. It was with great expectations I had begun them in Russia, that vast and alien[20] country, and when I now looked back on the many years I had worn the uniform of the Tsar, I had to admit with gratitude that my expectations had been fulfilled. I had entered into wider fields which had given me a broader vision than I could have had had I remained in Finland in the years around the turn of the century. I had been[21] fortunate in belonging to, and in commanding, crack troops with good officers and excellent morale. It had given me great satisfaction to command troops such as these, both in peace and war. Also I had seen so much of great interest in two continents.[22]

This reaction was quite understandable. A flattering biographer wrote of Mannerheim's arrival in St. Petersburg at the age of twenty: "And certainly, to a Finn, at the impressionable age of Gustaf Mannerheim in 1887, the whole was very strange, very wonderful: opening up, too, boundless fields for his ambition."[23] This ambition was fulfilled for Mannerheim as well as for many other Finnish officers in the Russian Army, although Mannerheim's personal ambitions, talents, and achievements were undoubtedly greater than most of his fellow officers. When he left his Uhlan regiment in early 1914 for wider responsibilities he told his men: "even though I am leaving you, I shall remain one of His Majesty's Uhlans until I die."[24] One night, early in World War I, his chief of staff awakened Mannerheim to inform the latter of a telegram from headquarters: Mannerheim could now wear the small white Cross of St. George, Fourth Class. "Oh, how happy I am!" repeated the wandering Finn. As he told his sister in a letter soon afterwards, "Now I can die happy."[25] If he had reached retirement age in the Russian Imperial Army, Mannerheim would indeed have died happy; that army, however, reached retirement age before he, and many of his fellow Finns, did.

In his later years the Marshal of Finland proudly displayed in his Helsinki home an autographed portrait of the last Emperor of Russia. When visitors expressed surprise Gustaf Mannerheim explained: "He was my Emperor."[26] This was not name dropping. Manner-

heim, having once taken an oath to Nicholas II, refused in 1917
to take an oath to the Russian Provisional Government and was
consequently removed from active duty in September of that
year.[27] Mannerheim's personal devotion to Nicholas II is entirely
understandable. The young Finn had been one of two Chevalier
Guards who, sword in hand, walked before the Emperor at the
ominously disastrous coronation of Nicholas II.[28] Upon his return
in 1909 to St. Petersburg from an intelligence mission to the border-
lands of the Russian and Chinese empires, Mannerheim reported
not only to the General Staff but to the Emperor privately.[29] After
his 1912 promotion to Major General à la suite of the Emperor,
Mannerheim had easy regular access to Nicholas II.[30] His last visit
to the Emperor was in mid-February 1917.[31] Mannerheim was in
fact a social companion of Nicholas II.

Mannerheim's attachment to Imperial Russia went far deeper
than personal loyalty to his wife or his Emperor, however. His
respect for the miracle, mystery, and authority of the Russian
Orthodox Church was great. A Lutheran by birth, he was overwhelmed by the Orthodox Easter.[32] Although he was never known
to his fellow Finns as a practicing Lutheran, Mannerheim was buried
in his great tomb in Helsinki with a gold cross, which he had long
carried next to his heart, in the Orthodox fashion.[33] Entirely appropriately, upon his death his former fellow officers in the Russian
Imperial Army held an Orthodox requiem mass in Paris for their
departed comrade-in-arms.[34] The Marshal of Finland may have
been buried in the Cemetery of Heroes in Helsinki, but Gustaf
Mannerheim was gently laid to rest in Paris.

The alienation from many other Finns of Finnish officers in the
Russian Imperial Army was particularly apparent during the Russo-
Japanese War and World War I. During the former war, Finnish
nationalists not only hoped for Russian defeat,[35] but secretly acquired
arms financed by the Japanese government.[36] At this moment,
Finnish officers were leading Russian troops into battle.[37] Mannerheim gave up a sinecure in St. Petersburg to volunteer for active
service in the war; as he left for the front, his fellow Chevalier Guards
presented their Lutheran friend with an Orthodox religious medal.[38]
Mannerheim's commanding general, Kuropatkin, was hated in
Finland as chief mover in the abolition of the Finnish Army.[39]

During World War I, members of the *Jäger* battalion fought against a Russian Imperial Army containing many Finnish officers.[40] It was the divergent experiences of these two generations of Finnish officers on the Eastern Front that was the fundamental barrier between them.[41] This barrier could never be removed.

Only the October Revolution in Russia forced the older generation of Finnish officers back to their homeland: "But when Bolshevism came to power in Russia, Mannerheim remembered that he had been born in Finland."[42] The roots of this generation of officers in Finland were far from deep. A member of the conservative Old Finnish parliamentary party described a meeting of his bloc on January 28, 1918—the day on which Gustaf Mannerheim, as Commander-in-Chief of the bourgeois Civil Guards, began the Finnish Civil War: "Who was Mannerheim? Not one member of the parliamentary bloc could give an answer."[43] A leading *Jäger* later spoke of Mannerheim's return to Finland as that of "a stranger come from a sunken world."[44] Writing of his departure for brief political exile in May 1918, after winning the Finnish Civil War, Mannerheim later recalled: "My departure from Finland presented me with no difficulties, since I possessed neither a home nor goods."[45]

Open conflict between these two generations of officers broke out immediately after the main body of *Jägers* landed in Finland in February 1918. The *Jägers* found themselves participants in a Finnish civil war on the side of the bourgeois Civil Guards—commanded by Mannerheim and other former Russian army officers—against the Social Democratic Red Guards. The *Jägers*, after discussions with German officers, decided to fight in Finland, as on the Eastern Front, as a separate unit, rather than to distribute themselves as officers among the Civil Guards. The *Jägers* thus hoped to avoid direct contact with the former Russian Imperial Army officers, "whose world view, especially concerning the struggle for independence, had earlier been so completely different."[46] Mannerheim refused to change his original plan to use the *Jägers* as officers throughout the poorly organized and led Civil Guards. The *Jägers* threatened to march the next morning to the front and begin fighting according to their own plan.[47] The strong will of the Commander-in-Chief nevertheless prevailed, and the *Jägers* were forced, with great dissatisfaction, to accept Mannerheim's decision.[48] During the course of the Finnish Civil War in 1918, the *Jägers* were prepared to take Mannerheim prisoner rather than serve in Eastern Finland under Major General Löfström, a former Russian Imperial Army officer.[49] Mannerheim recognized that all criticisms of former Russian Imperial Army officers by *Jägers* reflected upon him personally.[50] This recognition was shared by the *Jägers*; many years later, one of them spoke of Mannerheim's role in 1918: "To the *Jägers* he was a total stranger. He came from one camp, we from an entirely different one. We did not know him, and he did not know us."[51]

In the months immediately after the Finnish Civil War ended with the triumph of Mannerheim's White Army in May 1918, many more former officers in the Russian Imperial Army returned to Finland. For most of them, continuation of a military career seemed the only possible means of supporting themselves, especially since many of them had cut all financial ties to Finland in joining the Russian Imperial Army. The serious shortage of trained officers in the Finnish Army that was being created meant a warm welcome for them from the Commanding General of the Finnish Army, Wilkama, himself a former officer in the Russian Imperial Army. They were given at least the ranks they had held at the end of their service in the latter army. Since promotions had been relatively rapid in wartime, this meant that most of these former Russian officers received the most senior ranks. As colonels and generals in the Finnish Army, they met with intense disapproval[52] from those *Jägers* who decided after the Finnish Civil War upon military careers.[53] Wilkama opposed excessively rapid promotion of the latter. That his policy toward promotion did not seriously hinder the advance of the *Jägers* was apparent from the fact that half a decade after the Finnish Civil War the ablest of them were already colonels.[54] One *Jäger* became a major at twenty-one years of age, still a record in the Finnish Army.[55]

The *Jägers* engaged in private and sometimes personal guerrilla warfare against their superiors for several years.[56] Open conflict was probably inevitable,[57] and the disagreements between these two generations of officers eventually reached proportions that threatened the very existence of the Finnish defense establishment. In 1924 approximately 90 percent[58] of the officers in the Finnish Army, almost all of them *Jägers*, submitted their resignations en masse to dramatize their opposition to the older generation of former Russian Imperial Army officers. The *Jägers'* demand was nothing less than total victory:

(1) The removal from the defense establishment of all such elements whose patriotism is questionable or in whom Russian concepts, spirit, and habits have taken hold, as well as those who obviously have demonstrated themselves incompetent or are worthless because of their moral qualities. (2) The present army command, Generals Wilkama and Enckell, who are above all responsible for the Army's state of humiliation and towards whom the corps of officers does not feel confidence or adequate respect, are to be removed from their positions and replaced with better qualified men. . . . The corps of officers wishes by its resignation to demonstrate that its confidence in the present command has completely ended and that it does not consider itself able under the present command to carry that responsibility which falls to it while serving in the Army.[59]

Even *Jägers* conceded that these demands meant the complete collapse of military discipline.[60]

The strong support for Wilkama of K. J. Ståhlberg, President of the Republic,[61] together with the strong possibility that Wilkama would actually accept their resignations, forced most of the rebellious officers to retreat and to withdraw their resignations. Further weakening the position of the *Jägers* was the obvious falseness of at least some of their charges. The imputation of lack of moral principles might have been valid with respect to some of the most prominent strikers, but hardly with reference to Wilkama, a deeply religious man whose convictions were reflected in actions but seldom in words. Indeed, the strength of Wilkama's moral convictions was privately ridiculed by *Jägers*.[62] Quite possibly Wilkama was the Finnish soldier who, after Mannerheim, possessed the finest understanding of military strategy.[63] Enckell, a naval expert, had a high reputation in Russian military circles before his return to Finland.[64]

It soon became apparent that the *Jägers* had lost only a battle. The election to the presidency of Lauri Kristian Relander in 1925 resolved the conflict of generations within the Finnish Army. Relander was, from the beginning of his term, opposed to Wilkama.[65] The new President of the Republic felt—with considerable reason—intellectually inferior to the general.[66] Strong parliamentary and cabinet support for Wilkama delayed his removal for a short time. Finally, however, pressure from the Civil Guards[67]—Wilkama properly refused to cooperate with that organization[68]—was exerted against the general.[69] The Civil Guards considered President Relander their own man[70] since he was a leading and uncompromising member of that organization.[71] Relander did not fail the Civil Guards. While on an inspection tour of his troops Wilkama learned from a newspaper of his dismissal as Commanding General of the Finnish Army.[72] Not until the Winter War did this brilliant soldier again offer his services to the Finnish Army. Wilkama's successor was Major General Aarne Sihvo. At the age of thirty-six, this outstanding *Jäger* found himself at the peak of his military career. The Civil Guards found Sihvo much more acceptable than Wilkama. At least initially, Sihvo in his new position cooperated closely with the Civil Guards.[73] This cooperation was facilitated by the fact that the Commander of the Civil Guards was Lauri Malmberg, another *Jäger.*

Sihvo's promotion was the final blow to the position of the older generation of Finnish officers who had served in the Russian Imperial Army. The conflict of generations within the Finnish Army was resolved by the forced retreat of one of the combatants. The tenure of the older generation had proved short indeed.[74] From 1926 through World War II the top ranks of the Finnish Army were almost completely in the hands of *Jägers.* Of the sixteen Finnish generals on active duty in 1938 thirteen were *Jägers.*[75] During the Winter War almost all the important Finnish generals and colonels were *Jägers.*[76] Even some of those high-ranking officers who were not *Jägers* had become university students in 1917 and 1918, too late to participate in the *Jäger* movement.[77] Some of the non-*Jäger* commanders emulated *Jäger* traditions.[78] Only two Finnish generals—both artillery experts—during the Winter War had served in the Russian Imperial Army.[79] After the election of Gustaf Mannerheim to the office of President of the Republic in 1944, a *Jäger,* Erik Heinrichs, was his successor as Commander-in-Chief. Heinrich's generation had defeated its opponent, and won unchallenged control of the Finnish Army.

As is the case with all generational conflicts, however, victory—like the victors—was short-lived. Time was the ultimate vanquisher, and both generations of Finnish Army officers are today gone from that institution they commonly—if not together—created. The poet visiting the cemetery at Little Gidding, who did not write an elegy in a country churchyard, had it right:

These men, and those who opposed them
And those whom they opposed
Accept the constitution of silence
And are folded in a single party.[80]

What neither generation of Finnish officers realized was that both were necessary, and neither was by itself sufficient. What had to be created was an army that would serve an entire nation over many generations. Perhaps some day, when social conflict has been significantly reduced, in armies as everywhere else, human beings of different generations will see eye to eye. Since generational conflict is itself an important part of human conflict, such a reduction does not seem likely.

NOTES

1. Philippe Barres, *Charles De Gaulle* (Garden City, N.Y.: Doubleday, Doran and Company, 1941), p. 18; see also William Makepeace Thackeray, *Vanity Fair: A Novel Without a Hero* (New York: The New American Library, 1962), p. 274.

2. Vilho Tervasmäki, *Eduskuntaryhmät ja maanpuolustus valtiopäivillä 1917-1939* (Porvoo: Werner Söderström Osakeyhtiö, 1964).

3. The most famous Finn to serve as an officer in the Russian Imperial Army, Gustaf Mannerheim, was never *in* the Finnish Army. As an adolescent he had been expelled for disciplinary violations from the Finnish officer cadet school, after which he went to Russia. He was, during the Finnish Civil War of 1918, Commander-in-Chief of the Civil Guards; the Finnish Army was then nonexistent. Between 1919 and 1931 Mannerheim was not connected with the Finnish defense establishment. In the latter year he became Chairman of the Defense Council, and at the beginning of the Winter War he became Commander-in-Chief, in accordance with the constitutional provision authorizing the President of the Republic to delegate his position as Commander-in-Chief to someone else during wartime. Thus constitutionally Mannerheim's position in the Winter War and World War II was *above* the Finnish Army. The legal position of Mannerheim in

the period of peace between March 1940 and June 1941 has never been clarified.

4. Ulrich von Coler, "Jääkäripataljoona," in *Suomen vapaussota I: Valmistelut ja esihistoria*, ed. Kai Donner, Th. Svedlin, and Heikki Nurmio (Jyväskylä: K. J. Gummerus Osakeyhtiö, 1921), p. 135.

5. Ibid., p. 138; see also Paavo Rintala, *Nahkapeitturien linjalla I: Romaani* (Helsinki: Kustannusosakeyhtiö Otava, 1976), pp. 212-13.

6. Matti Lauerma, "Suomalainen vapaustaistelija vaiko preussilainen jääkäri?" *Historiallinen aikakauskirja*, 1963, p. 110.

7. At first many of the *Jägers* demanded that the German military command explicitly promise they would be used against Russian troops. The German military command, however, considered that such a promise on its part would be incompatible with military discipline. A. R. Cederberg, *Suomen uusinta historiaa 1898-1942* (Porvoo: Werner Söderström Osakeyhtiö, 1943), p. 148.

8. Coler, "Jääkäripataljoona," p. 150; Axel Grönvik, *Kenraaleja ja kenttäeverstejä*, trans. J. A. Wecksell (Helsinki: Kustannusosakeyhtiö Otava, 1940), p. 9; M. Rantavuori and Kosti Karakoski, *Maanpuolustus: maanpuolustusopetuken käsikirja* (Porvoo: Werner Söderström Osakeyhtiö, 1939), p. 136.

9. Juhani Paasivirta, *Suomi vuonna 1918* (Porvoo: Werner Söderström Osakeyhtiö, 1957), p. 194.

10. At the end of 1916 a Finnish-language newspaper was established by *Jäger* battalion members. In the first issue a feeling of comradeship, both of being isolated from everyone else, and of complete dependence on each other, is given as the reason for founding the newspaper. "Suomen Jääkärin lukijoille," *Suomen Jääkäri*, December 30, 1916.

11. Tönnies's classic work appeared as *Fundamental Concepts of Sociology (Gemeinschaft und Gesellschaft)*, trans. and suppl. Charles P. Loomis (New York: American Book Company, 1940).

12. This second *Waffenbrüderschaft* included the presence of Finnish troops on the Eastern Front in what became the *SS-Panzer-grenadier-Division Wiking*. These troops, who were permitted by the Finnish government to begin their secret journey to Germany seven weeks before both Germany and Finland were at war with the Soviet Union, clearly conceived of their presence in the German Army as a renewal of the experience of the *Jägers*. Unto Parvilahti, *Terekille ja takaisin: Suomalaisen vapaaehtoisjoukon vaiheita Saksan itärintamalla 1941-43* (Helsinki: Kustannusosakeyhtiö Otava, 1959), pp. 7, 10, 19-20, 23-25, 37, 83, 90, 114-15, 138-39, 232, 235-37, 241, 262, 264, 292, 295; Mauno Jokipii, *Panttipataljoona: Suomalaisen SS-pataljoonan historia* (Helsinki: Weilin & Göös, 1969), pp. 65, 369, 371.

13. W. E. Tuompo, *Sotilaan tilinpäätös* (Porvoo: Werner Söderström Osakeyhtiö, 1967), p. 75; Hugo Österman, *Neljännesvuosisata elämästäni* (Porvoo: Werner Söderström Osakeyhtiö, 1966), pp. 12-13; Alan Cassels, *Fascism* (Arlington Heights, Ill.: AHM Publishing Corporation, 1975), p. 226. The last *Jäger* retired from the Finnish defense establishment in 1960. *Helsingin Sanomat*, February 26, 1961, p. 17. Surprisingly, this was two years after the last member of the first class of the Finnish Military Academy (founded in 1919) left active service. Leo Franck, *Ensimmäinen kadettikurssi*, trans. Vesa Santavuori (Hämeenlinna: Arvi A. Karisto Osakeyhtiö, 1969), p. 139.

14. Paavo Talvela, *Sotilaan elämä: Muistelmat*, vol. I, ed. Vilho Tervasmäki and Sampo Ahto (Jyväskylä: Kirjayhtymä, 1976), p. 8.

15. L. A. Puntila, *The Political History of Finland 1809-1966*, trans. David Miller (Helsinki: The Otava Publishing Co., 1974), p. 29; L. G. Beskrovnyi, *Russkaia armiia i flot v XIX veke* (Moscow: Izdatel'stvo 'Nauka,' 1973), p. 61; John Shelton Curtiss, *The Russian Army under Nicholas I, 1825-1855* (Durham, N. C.: Duke University Press, 1965), p. 207.

16. Beskrovnyi, *Russkaia armiia i flot v XIX veke*, p. 8; Curtiss, *The Russian Army under Nicholas I*, p. 211; M. K. Dziewanowski, *Joseph Pilsudski: A European Federalist, 1918-1922* (Stanford: Hoover Institution Press, 1969), p. 53.

17. Carl Enckell, *Poliitset Muistelmani*, vol. I, trans. Heikki Impola (Porvoo: Werner Söderström Osakeyhtiö, 1956), p. 14.

18. Matti Alajoki, *Tykistönkenraali Vilho Petter Nenonen* (Helsinki: Kustannusosakeyhtiö Otava, 1975), p. 56.

19. Ibid., p. 63.

20. To describe Imperial Russia as "alien" was perhaps a conscious deception by the aged Marshal of Finland. When, as a young officer, Mannerheim married a Russian woman, he wrote to his relatives in Finland that Russia was "our great Fatherland." Stig Jägerskiöld, *Nuori Mannerheim*, trans. Sirkka Rapola (Helsinki: Kustannusosakeyhtiö Otava, 1964), p. 105. The young Mannerheim was the real Mannerheim.

21. Mannerheim's last command as a Lieutenant General in the Russian Army was the Sixth Cavalry Army Corps in Transylvania.

22. *The Memoirs of Marshal Mannerheim*, trans. Count Eric Lewenhaupt (London: Cassell, 1953), p. 124.

23. Tancred Borenius, *Field-Marshal Mannerheim* (London: Hutchinson, 1940), p. 19.

24. Stig Jägerskiöld, *Gustaf Mannerheim 1906-1917*, trans. Sirkka Rapola (Helsinki: Kustannusosakeyhtiö Otava, 1965), p. 145.

25. Ibid., p. 198.

26. Yrjö Niiniluoto, *Suuri rooli: Suomen marsalkan, vapaaherra Carl Gustaf Mannerheimin kirjallisen muotokuvan yritelmä* (Helsinki: Kustannusosakeyhtiö Otava, 1962), p. 33.

27. Jägerskiöld, *Gustaf Mannerheim 1906-1917*, pp. 387-89.

28. J. E. O. Screen, *Mannerheim: The Years of Preparation* (London: C. Hurst & Company, 1970), p. 36; Borenius, *Field-Marshal Mannerheim*, p. 21; *The Memoirs of Marshal Mannerheim*, p. 11; Paul Rodzianko, *Mannerheim: An Intimate Picture of a Great Soldier and Statesman* (London: Jarrolds, 1940), p. 54.

29. Screen, *Mannerheim*, p. 83.

30. Ibid., p. 95.

31. Ibid., p. 112.

32. *The Memoirs of Marshal Mannerheim*, p. 10; Rodzianko, *Mannerheim*, pp. 30-31, 98.

33. Niiniluoto, *Suuri rooli*, pp. 73-74; Gustaf Ehrnrooth, "Carl Gustaf Emil Mannerheim: Muistopuhe," in Suomen Aatelisliitto, *Suomen Marsalkka Vapaaherra Gustaf Mannerheim: Sotilas—Valtiomies—Ihminen* (Helsinki: Kustannusosakeyhtiö Otava, 1953), p. 32.

34. Anni Voipio, *Suomen Marsalkka: elämäkerta* (Porvoo: Werner Söderström Osakeyhtiö, 1953), p. 405.

35. Wihtori Kosola, *Viimeistä piirtoa myöten: muistelmia elämäni varrelta* (Lapua: Lapuan kirjapaino, 1935), p. 57; Herman Gummerus, in *P. E. Svinhufvud 1861-1936*, ed. Juhlatoimikunta (Helsinki: Kustannusosakeyhtiö Otava), pp. 11, 15; Jägerskiöld, *Nuori Mannerheim*, pp. 292-93; S. Galai, "The Impact of War on the Russian Liberals in 1904-5," *Government and Opposition* 1 (November 1965): 89, 101.

36. Eino I. Parmanen, *Taistelujen kirja: kuvauksia itsenäisyystaistelumme vaiheista sortovuosina: III osa: taistelun ja jännityksen aikaa: rajuilma yltymässä myrskyksi* (Porvoo: Werner Söderström Osakeyhtiö, 1939), pp. 286-87, 334-35, 661-77; K. G. Idman, *Maamme itsenäistymisen vuosilta: Muistelmia* (Porvoo: Werner Söderström Osakeyhtiö, 1953), p. 22; Kalle Väänänen, *Vainotien vartijat: Etelä-Karjalan maanpuolustushistoriaa* (Viipuri: Viipurin suojeluskuntapiirin piiriesikunta, 1939), p. 26; Gummerus, in Juhlatoimikunta, ed., *P. E. Svinhufvud*, p. 9.

37. *The Memoirs of Marshal Mannerheim*, pp. 19-21; Väinö Haapanen, *Upseerielämää: Muistikuvia suomalaisen armeijaupseerin palvelusajalta Venäjällä* (Helsinki: Kustannusosakeyhtiö Otava, 1928), pp. 90-148.

38. Jägerskiöld, *Nuori Mannerheim*, p. 312.

39. Borenius, *Field-Marshal Mannerheim*, p. 32.

40. *The Memoirs of Marshal Mannerheim*, pp. 80-109; Haapanen, *Upseerielämää*, pp. 209-37; Aino Ackté-Jalander, *Kenraali Bruno Jalanderin muistelmia Kaukaasiasta ja Suomen murroskaudelta* (Helsinki: Kustannuso-

---

sakeyhtiö Otava, 1932), pp. 147-60; Väinö Tanner, *Näin Helsingin kasvavan* (Helsinki: Kustannusosakeyhtiö Tammi, 1949), pp. 265, 267.

41. Paasivirta, *Suomi vuonna 1918*, p. 233.

42. Wipert v. Blücher, *Suomen kohtalonaikoja: Muistelmia vuosilta 1935-44*, trans. Lauri Hirvensalo (Porvoo: Werner Söderström Osakeyhtiö, 1950), p. 239. Mannerheim's return—in December 1917—occurred after a trip from Odessa to Petrograd in a private railroad car. Mannerheim was wearing the full dress uniform of an Imperial Army Corps Commander. Erkki Räikkönen, *Svinhufvud ja itsenäisyyssenaatti: piirteitä P. E. Svinhufvudin ja hänen johtamansa senaatin toiminnasta ja vaiheista syksyllä 1917 ja keväällä 1918* (Helsinki: Kustannusosakeyhtiö Otava, 1935), pp. 217-18; Rodzianko, *Mannerheim*, p. 118; Borenius, *Field-Marshal Mannerheim*, pp. 68-69; Martin Franck, "Hussarin muistelmia kenraali Mannerheimista ensimmäisen maailmansodan ajoilta," in Suomen Aatelisliitto, *Suomen Marsalkka*, p. 98.

43. Paavo Virkkunen, *Kahden sataluvun vaiheilta: elettyä ja ajateltua* (Helsinki: Kustannusosakeyhtiö Otava, 1953), p. 320.

44. Erik Heinrichs, *Mannerheim Suomen kohtaloissa: I: Valkoinen kenraali 1918-1919* (Helsinki: Kustannusosakeyhtiö Otava, 1957), p. 17.

45. *The Memoirs of Marshal Mannerheim*, p. 184.

46. Räikkönen, *Svinhufvud*, pp. 347-48.

47. Ibid., p. 349; Paasivirta, *Suomi vuonna 1918*, p. 199n; Aarne Sihvo, *Muistelmani*, vol. I (Helsinki: Kustannusosakeyhtiö Otava, 1954), p. 357.

48. Räikkönen, *Svinhufvud*, p. 362; Talvela, *Sotilaan elämä*, vol. I, p. 57; Alajoki, *Tykistönkenraali Vilho Petter Nenonen*, p. 98; Paasivirta, *Suomi vuonna 1918*, p. 199. Three decades later, the Commander-in-Chief ignored the essence of this dispute. *The Memoirs of Marshal Mannerheim*, p. 152.

49. Letter of Rudolf Walden to his wife, April 13, 1918, cited by Einar W. Juva, *Rudolf Walden 1878-1946* (Porvoo: Werner Söderström Osakeyhtiö, 1957), p. 105.

50. Heinrichs, *Mannerheim Suomen kohtaloissa*, vol. I, p. 80. Mannerheim during World War II opposed the presence of Finnish troops in the *SS-Panzer-grenadier-Division Wiking*. *The Memoirs of Marshal Mannerheim*, pp. 466-67; Parvilahti, *Terekille ja takaisin*, pp. 138, 144-45, 269-71; Blücher, *Suomen kohtalonaikoja*, p. 301.

51. Tuompo, *Sotilaan tilinpäätös*, p. 80.

52. Aarne Sihvo, *Muistelmani*, vol. II (Helsinki: Kustannusosakeyhtiö Otava, 1956), p. 87; Lauri Hyvämäki, *Sinistä ja mustaa: Tutkielmia Suomen oikestoradikalismista* (Helsinki: Kustannusosakeyhtiö Otava, 1971), p. 10.

53. Paavo Virkkunen, *Itsenäisen Suomen alkuvuosikymmeniltä: elettyä ja ajateltua* (Helsinki: Kustannusosakeyhtiö Otava, 1954), p. 221.

54. Ibid. Perhaps expectably, Finnish military aviation appears to have avoided this conflict almost entirely, judging from Armas Eskola, *Lentäminen oli välttmätöntä: sotilasilmailua rauhan ja sodan aikana* (Hämeenlinna: Arvi A. Karisto Osakeyhtiö, 1969).

55. Talvela, *Sotilaan elämä*, vol. I, p. 9.

56. Ibid., pp. 58-60.

57. Ibid., p. 9.

58. Ibid., p. 61.

59. This document is reprinted in Virkkunen, *Itsenäisen Suomen alkuvuosikymmeniltä*, pp. 223-24.

60. Sihvo, *Muistelmani*, vol. II, p. 39.

61. Virkkunen, *Itsenäisen Suomen alkuvuosikymmeniltä*, pp. 228, 233, 238-39.

62. Lauri Malmberg, cited by Sihvo, *Muistelmani*, vol. II, p. 241.

63. Virkkunen, *Itsenäisen Suomen alkuvuosikymmeniltä*, p. 232.

64. Idman, *Maamme itsenäistymisen vuosilta*, p. 343; Juho Niukkanen, *Talvisodan puolustusministeri kertoo* (Porvoo: Werner Söderström Osakeyhtiö, 1951), p. 22.

65. Virkkunen, *Itsenäisen Suomen alkuvuosikymmeniltä*, p. 230; Eino Jutikkala, ed., *Presidentin päiväkirja: I: Lauri Kristian Relanderin muistiinpanot vuosilta 1925-1927* (Helsinki: Weilin & Göös, 1967), pp. 37-38, 50-54, 63-64.

66. Virkkunen, *Itsenäisen Suomen alkuvuosikymmeniltä*, p. 241.

67. The victorious bourgeois army of the Finnish Civil War was not disbanded after 1918, even after a national army was created. The primary purpose of the Civil Guards organization after 1918 was to keep the victory of that year intact. For the problems that the continued existence of this state within a state caused for the Finnish political system, see Marvin Rintala, *Three Generations: The Extreme Right Wing in Finnish Politics* (Bloomington: Indiana University, 1962).

68. Sihvo, *Muistelmani*, vol. II, p. 120; Jutikkala, ed., *Presidentin päiväkirja*, vol. I, pp. 134, 191, 195, 198, 211, 282.

69. Sihvo, *Muistelmani*, vol. II, pp. 108, 122; Kosola, *Viimeistä piirtoa myöten*, p. 201; Virkkunen, *Itsenäisen Suomen alkuvuosikymmeniltä*, p. 244; Jutikkala, ed., *Presidentin päiväkirja*, vol. I, pp. 91-92, 197.

70. Sihvo, *Muistelmani*, vol. II, p. 121.

71. Väänänen, *Vainotien vartijat*, pp. 223-24, 226; Jutikkala, ed., *Presidentin päiväkirja*, vol. I, pp. 71, 88-89, 118-19, 121, 134, 191, 197.

72. Virkkunen, *Itsenäisen Suomen alkuvuosikymmeniltä*, pp. 243-44.

73. Sihvo, *Muistelmani*, vol. II, p. 125.

74. Puntila, *The Political History of Finland 1809-1966*, p. 138; Matti

Lauerma, *Kuninkaallinen Preussin Jääkäripataljoona 27: vaiheet ja vaikutus* (Porvoo: Werner Söderström Osakeyhtiö, 1966), p. 940.

75. Antero Krekola, "Sotilaseliitti Suomessa," *Politiikka* 10 (1968): 20.

76. Stig Jägerskiöld, *Talvisodan ylipäällikkö: Sotamarsalkka Gustaf Mannerheim 1939-1941*, trans. Kai Kaila (Helsinki: Kustannusosakeyhtiö Otava, 1976), pp. 33-34. They included Edvard Hanell, Erik Heinrichs, Juho Heiskanen, Woldemar Hägglund,Taavetti Laatikainen, Jarl Lundqvist, Lauri Malmberg, Karl Lennart Oesch, Aarne Sihvo, Hjalmar Siilasvuo, Paavo Talvela, Viljo Tuompo, Väinö Valve, Harald Öhquist, and Hugo Österman. Biographical material concerning these *Jägers* is given by: Grönvik, *Kenraaleja ja kenttäeverstejä*, pp. 7-39, 45-60, 66-68; H. R. Söderström and J. O. Tallqvist, eds., *Vem och vad? Biografisk handbok 1941* (Helsingfors: Holger Schildts Förlag, 1941), pp. 202, 219-21, 262-63, 363, 408, 419, 472, 595-96, 650, 677, 698, 755, 758-59.

77. The most important of these was Aksel Airo, whose biography is given by Söderström and Tallqvist, eds., *Vem och vad? 1941*, p. 13. An entirely unsatisfactory attempt to explain this enigmatic man is Erkki Salometsä, *A. F. Airo: vaikeneva kenraali* (Hämeenlinna: Arvi A. Karisto Osakeyhtiö, 1970). Virtually all interwar Finnish university students who considered military careers were enthusiasts of the *Jägers'* cause. Martti Santavuori, "Näkymiä 1920-ja 1930 luvuilta—lähinnä maanpuolustuksen kannalta," in *Ilon ja aatteen vuodet*, ed. Toini Havu (Hämeenlinna: Arvi A. Karisto Osakeyhtiö, 1965), p. 82.

78. Lauri Kulmala, " 'Sotahullu' ja pelätty Pajari 'sammakkoperspektiivistä' " in *Pajari rintamakenraali: Aaro Olavi Pajari (1897-1949) sotilaana, esimiehenä ja ihmisenä*, ed. Jukka Tyrkkö (Helsinki: Kustannusosakeyhtiö Otava, 1974), pp. 190-91.

79. Biographies of these two, Vilho Nenonen and Väinö Svanström, are given by: Söderström and Tallqvist, eds., *Vem och vad? 1941*, pp. 445, 639-40; Grönvik, *Kenraaleja ja kenttäeverstejä*, pp. 40-44.

80. T. S. Eliot, *The Complete Poems and Plays 1909-1950* (New York: Harcourt, Brace & World, 1971), p. 143.

Essay 4

The Literature of Generations

GENERATIONS: KEY TO POLITICS?

The intellectual history of the concept of generations is woven from two separate strands. The first of these strands is primarily analytical, detached, and social scientific. The second is primarily impressionistic, passionate, and humanistic. The first strand is like a cold, hard steel wire, capable of encompassing and perhaps even lifting a heavy empirical load, but also capable of cutting badly into human flesh if one is not careful around it. The second strand is like a unique string of pearls, lovely but useful only in the right circumstances. The first strand has much instrumental value as a tool of understanding, but as a prosaic thing has little inherent value, especially when, as in its origins, its concepts are articulated in clumsy language. The second strand is a thing of beauty, inspiring in itself, especially when, as in its origins, its insights are advanced with literary eloquence, but difficult to apply in a wide variety of social circumstances. Some would call the first strand Germanic and the other strand Hispanic. The present author, being a social scientist, must prefer the applicable to the ethereal, but not all readers need agree, and even a preference for the former need not blind one to the attractiveness of the latter.

The *alpha,* if one may hope, not the *omega,* of the first strand is, of course, Karl Mannheim. The classic expression of Mannheim's theory of generations is his "The Problem of Generations," in his *Essays on the Sociology of Knowledge,* ed. Paul Kecskemeti (London:

Routledge and Kegan Paul Ltd., 1952), pp. 276-320. This essay, difficult and opaque, has often been misunderstood. Written in 1927, it was never revised into a simpler form by its author. Much more intelligible are statements of generations theory by two distinguished scholars with a clear insight into Mannheim's argument: Sigmund Neumann, *Permanent Revolution: Totalitarianism in the Age of International Civil War*, 2nd ed. (New York: Frederick A. Praeger, 1965), pp. 230-56; Rudolf Heberle, "The Problem of Political Generations," in his *Social Movements: An Introduction to Political Sociology* (New York: Appleton-Century-Crofts, 1951), pp. 118-27. The analytical perspective of another, later, generation is found in: Marvin Rintala, "A Generation in Politics: A Definition," *The Review of Politics* 25 (October 1963):509-22; Marvin Rintala, "Political Generations," *International Encyclopedia of the Social Sciences*, vol. VI, (1968), pp. 92-96.

The second strand of the intellectual history of the concept of generations begins with José Ortega y Gasset: *Man and Crisis*, trans. Mildred Adams (New York: W. W. Norton & Company, 1962), pp. 30-84; *The Modern Theme*, trans. James Cleugh (New York: Harper & Brothers, 1961), pp. 11-18. The function of clarification, performed briliantly for Mannheim by Neumann and Heberle, has been performed equally well for Ortega y Gasset by Julián Marías: *Generations: A Historical Method*, trans. Harold C. Raley (University, Ala.: The University of Alabama Press, 1970); "Generations: The Concept," *International Encyclopedia of the Social Sciences*, vol. VI, (1968), pp. 88-92. The significance of the concept of generation in the thought of Ortega y Gasset is stressed in two valuable biographies: Julián Marías, *José Ortega y Gasset: Circumstance and Vocation*, trans. Frances M. López-Morillas (Norman: University of Oklahoma Press, 1970); Harold C. Raley, *José Ortega y Gasset: Philosopher of European Unity* (University, Ala.: The University of Alabama Press, 1971).

There is no satisfactory intellectual biography of Mannheim, perhaps not surprisingly in view of his personality, but there are some case studies of political generations applying Mannheim's approach: Maurice Zeitlin, "Political Generations in the Cuban Working Class," *The American Journal of Sociology* 71 (March 1966): 493-508; Maurice Zeitlin, *Revolutionary Politics and the*

Cuban Working Class (New York: Harper & Row, 1970), pp. 211-41; Marvin Rintala, *Three Generations: The Extreme Right Wing in Finnish Politics* (Bloomington: Indiana University, 1962); Marvin Rintala, "Finland," in *The European Right: A Historical Profile*, ed. Hans Rogger and Eugen Weber (Berkeley: University of California Press, 1965), pp. 408-41; Marvin Rintala, "Äärioikeisto Suomen poliittisessa elämässä 1917-1939," *Politiikka* 5 (1963): 87-112, 132-33; Marvin Rintala, "The Problem of Generations in Finnish Communism," *The American Slavic and East European Review* 17 (April 1958): 190-202; Marvin Rintala, "Suomen kommunismin sukupolviongelmat," *Sosiologia*, 1964, pp. 149-56. There are also some political biographies applying Mannheim's approach to generations. Such efforts include: Marvin Rintala, "Väinö Tanner in Finnish Politics," *The American Slavic and East European Review* 20 (February 1961): 84-98; Marvin Rintala, "The Politics of Gustaf Mannerheim," *Journal of Central European Affairs* 21 (April 1961): 67-83; Marvin Rintala, *Four Finns: Political Profiles* (Berkeley: University of California Press, 1969); Edgar Alexander, "The Dilemma: The Generations' Problem," in his *Adenauer and the New Germany: The Chancellor of the Vanquished*, trans. Thomas E. Goldstein (New York: Farrar, Straus and Cudahy, 1957), pp. 33-42.

There are, to the present writer's knowledge, no political scientific case studies attempting to apply the concept of generation of Ortega y Gasset, and it is difficult to imagine how this might be done. Less Mannheimian, if also non-Ortegan, but interesting case studies of political generations include: Raymond A. Bauer, Alex Inkeles, and Clyde Kluckhohn, "Generational Differences," in their *How the Soviet System Works: Cultural, Psychological, and Social Themes* (Cambridge: Harvard University Press, 1956), pp. 190-98; Leopold H. Haimson, "Three Generations of the Soviet Intelligentsia," *Foreign Affairs* 37 (January 1959): 235-46; Borys Lewytzkyj, "Generations in Conflict," *Problems of Communism* 16 (January-February 1967): 36-40; Merle Fainsod, "Soviet Youth and the Problem of the Generations," *Proceedings of the American Philosophical Society* 108 (October 1964): 429-36; Stan A. Taylor and Robert S. Wood, "Image and Generation: A Social-Psychological Analysis of the Sino-Soviet Dispute," *Brigham Young University Studies* 7:143-58.

Some of the more important contributions to a sociology of generations are: Donald G. MacRae, "The Culture of a Generation: Students and Others," *The Journal of Contemporary History* 2 (July 1967):3-13; Lewis S. Feuer, *The Conflict of Generations: The Character and Significance of Student Movements* (New York: Basic Books, 1969); S. N. Eisenstadt, *From Generation to Generation: Age Groups and Social Structure* (Glencoe, Ill.: The Free Press, 1956); S. N. Eisenstadt and J. Ben-David, "Inter-Generation Tensions in Israel," *International Social Science Bulletin* 8 (1956): 54-75; William M. Evan, "Cohort Analysis of Survey Data: A Procedure for Studying Long-term Opinion Change," *Public Opinion Quarterly* 23 (1959): 62-72; Ben Halpern, *The Idea of the Jewish State* (Cambridge: Harvard University Press, 1961); Joseph R. Gusfield, "The Problem of Generations in an Organizational Structure," *Social Forces* 35 (May 1957): 323-30; Bennett M. Berger, "How Long is a Generation?" *The British Journal of Sociology* 11 (March 1960): 10-23; Alex Simirenko, "Mannheim's generational analysis and acculturation," *The British Journal of Sociology* 17 (September 1966): 292-99; Gosta [*sic*] Carlsson and Katarina Karlsson, "Age, Cohorts and the Generation of Generations," *American Sociological Review* 35 (August 1970): 710-18.

THE EUROPEAN WAR GENERATION OF 1914-18

The written remains of the war generation are enormous, almost approaching in magnitude the number of graves left by the Great War. Even many of the missing voices left their literary testaments. No other war has produced so much poetry and imaginative fiction, some of it of a terrible beauty. Each reader can ascertain from the text and footnotes which particular authors among the diversity of the war generation might prove most meaningful to that reader, and that preference is likely to reveal something rather essential about that reader's perception of the human condition. Choosing among these authors is intimately, almost indecently, personal. This particular reader will therefore merely suggest a few options, with the hope of remaining neutral among the different generation units of the war generation. Each of those units can speak for itself. Therefore no attempt—with only two exceptions, one musical—

will be made to recommend works that are traditionally called secondary sources, which in the present context are works by nonmembers of the war generation. These secondary sources are also numerous, since writing about the war generation has itself become virtually a cottage industry, and some of them are works of distinction, but they are perhaps already enumerated sufficiently in footnotes. The standard of evaluation most appropriate here, furthermore, is not some arbitrary criterion of literary excellence, but rather: where can one learn most readily about the inner realities of the experience, and the experiences, of the war generation?

Quite probably the most eloquent of the missing voices is found in C. Day Lewis, ed., *The Collected Poems of Wilfred Owen* (New York: New Directions, 1964). Owen's poetry, interspersed with the *Missa pro Defunctis*, provides the text for Benjamin Britten's masterpiece, the *War Requiem*, Opus 66 (London Records OSA 1255). Equally probably, as already suggested, the classic literary statement of the apolitical response to the Great War is made in *The Poems of Edmund Blunden 1914-1930* (London: Cobden-Sanderson, 1930). The pacific response is still most powerfully articulated in Erich Maria Remarque, *All Quiet on the Western Front* (New York: Crest Books, 1964), whose overwhelming popular success should not be held against it. The militant response is most clearly set forth in Ernst Jünger, *On the Marble Cliffs*, trans. Stuart Hood (Harmondsworth, Eng.: Penguin Books, 1970). The most extended fictional account of the experiences of the war generation is Henry Williamson's series of novels with the overall title "A Chronicle of Ancient Sunlight." Perhaps the most searing account of the front experience in this vast series is *The Golden Virgin* (London: Macdonald, 1966), and the most explicitly political in theme is *The Phoenix Generation* (London: Macdonald, 1965). Williamson's novels are important for much more than their total length. The missing voices and the apolitical, pacific, and militant responses are all treated with a dignity that is impressive. The tone of "A Chronicle of Ancient Sunlight" is much less bitter than that of Williamson's *The Patriot's Progress: Being the Vicissitudes of Pte. John Bullock* (London: Macdonald, 1968), which has appropriately incisive linocut illustrations by William Kermode.

Moving from poetry and imaginative fiction to more prosaic, but not necessarily more instructive, writings, the most intellectually impressive statement of the apolitical response is Herbert Read, *Anarchy and Order: Essays in Politics* (Boston: Beacon Press, 1971), which should be read in conjunction with Herbert Read, *The Contrary Experience: autobiographies* (London: Faber and Faber, 1963) for fullest understanding. The pacific response pervades Hugh Dalton, *Towards the Peace of Nations: A Study in International Politics* (London: George Routledge & Sons, Ltd., 1928). Ironically, however, the most important statement of the pacific response is found in the two-volume autobiography of that member of the war generation who knew the most about the strategies of war: *The Memoirs of Captain Liddell Hart* (London: Cassell, 1965). Liddell Hart's memoirs may not be the ideal place to start learning about the war generation, but the incisive mind and mastery of fact unfailingly present in those memoirs make them an indispensable source to serious students of the war generation. The most important expressions of the militant response are Adolf Hitler, *Mein Kampf*, trans. Ralph Manheim (Boston: Houghton Mifflin Company, 1943) and Charles de Gaulle, *The Edge of the Sword*, trans. Gerard Hopkins (New York: Criterion Books, 1960). There is a broad panorama of recollections by members of the war generation in George A. Panichas, ed., *Promise of Greatness: The War of 1914-1918* (New York: The John Day Company, 1968).

In both human and scholarly terms, one book by a student of the war generation towers above all the rest: Martin Middlebrook, *The First Day on the Somme: 1 July 1916* (Glasgow: Fontana/Collins, 1975). All the major themes of the war generation are there, developed with an excellent sense of proportion, making Middlebrook's book the most appropriate single place for the aspiring student of the war generation to begin. That this superb study is so relatively recent should encourage beginning students to hope that there is still room at the top.

GENERATIONAL CONFLICT
WITHIN THE FINNISH ARMY

Some helpful biographies or autobiographies of Finnish officers who served in the Russian Imperial Army are: Matti Alajoki,

Tykistönkenraali Vilho Petter Nenonen (Helsinki: Kustannusosakeyhtiö Otava, 1975); Väinö Haapanen, *Upseerielämää: Muistikuvia suomalaisen armeijaupseerin palvelusajalta Venäjällä* (Helsinki: Kustannusosakeyhtiö Otava, 1928); Aino Ackté-Jalander,
*Kenraali Bruno Jalanderin muistelmia Kaukaasiasta ja Suomen
murroskaudelta* (Helsinki: Kustannusosakeyhtiö Otava, 1932).
The literature on this generation of Finnish officers is inevitably
dominated by the mountain of biographies of Gustaf Mannerheim.
There are more books about him than about any other Finn. Unfortunately their quality does not match their quantity. The fatal
flaw of most of them is that the three decades Mannerheim spent in
the Russian Imperial Army are ignored. This is even essentially
true of a two-volume study by the *Jäger* who in 1944 succeeded
Mannerheim as Commander-in-Chief of the Finnish Army, Erik
Heinrichs, *Mannerheim Suomen kohtaloissa* (Helsinki: Kustannusosakeyhtiö Otava, 1957 and 1959), which is otherwise reliable,
and is especially interesting on military matters. Only the first two
volumes are essential of an inflated life and times of Mannerheim,
presently in six volumes and still growing, by Stig Jägerskiöld,
Nuori Mannerheim and *Gustaf Mannerheim 1906-1917*, trans.
Sirkka Rapola (Helsinki: Kustannusosakeyhtiö Otava, 1964 and
1965). In these first two volumes Jägerskiöld, a distant relative
of Mannerheim, has been able to draw upon valuable family docu-
ments, but his later volumes virtually ignore the young and middle-
aged Mannerheim presented in the first two volumes. The lack of
psychological emphasis in Jägerskiöld and most other biographers
of Mannerheim is at least compensated for in an impressive psycho-
biography by a Finnish journalist, Yrjö Niiniluoto, *Suuri rooli:
Suomen marsalkan, vapaaherra Carl Gustaf Mannerheimin kirjallisen muotokuvan yritelmä* (Helsinki: Kustannusosakeyhtiö Otava,
1962). Mannerheim lies on the couch for an even more extended
session in three novels by Paavo Rintala: *Mummoni ja Mannerheim, Mummoni ja Marsalkka*, and *Mummoni ja Marskin tarinat*
(Helsinki: Kustannusosakeyhtiö Otava, 1960, 1961, and 1962). An
analytical, but not psychoanalytical, interpretation of Mannerheim
is found in: Marvin Rintala, "The Politics of Gustaf Mannerheim,"
Journal of Central European Affairs 21 (April 1961):67-83; Marvin
Rintala, *Four Finns: Political Profiles* (Berkeley: University of

California Press, 1969), pp. 13-46. The best book-length biography of Mannerheim, appropriately confined to his years in the Russian Imperial Army, is J. E. O. Screen, *Mannerheim: The Years of Preparation* (London: C. Hurst & Company, 1970). The only defect in Screen's distinguished study is its title; the years before 1918 were not merely a period of preparation for Mannerheim, but a peak of achievement that he never surpassed in his own estimation, as is apparent in one of the many monuments Mannerheim planned for himself: *The Memoirs of Marshal Mannerheim*, trans. Count Eric Lewenhaupt (London: Cassell, 1953).

Standard autobiographies by representative *Jägers* include a first volume by Paavo Talvela, *Sotilaan elämä: Muistelmat*, ed. Vilho Tervasmäki and Sampo Ahto (Jyväskylä: Kirjayhtymä, 1976); W. E. Tuompo, *Sotilaan tilinpäätös* (Porvoo: Werner Söderström Osakeyhtiö, 1967); Hugo Österman, *Neljännesvuosisata elämästäni* (Porvoo: Werner Söderström Osakeyhtiö, 1966). The most important memoirs of a *Jäger* are the two volumes by Aarne Sihvo, *Muistelmani* (Helsinki: Kustannusosakeyhtiö Otava, 1954 and 1956). A competent historical study of the *Jäger* experience is by Matti Lauerma, *Kuninkaallinen Preussin Jääkäripataljoona 27: vaiheet ja vaikutus* (Porvoo: Werner Söderström Osakeyhtiö, 1966). There is as yet no analogous general published study of Finnish officers in the Russian Imperial Army.

A valuable reference work about both generations of Finnish officers is Axel Grönvik, *Kenraaleja ja kenttäeverstejä*, trans. J. A. Wecksell (Helsinki: Kustannusosakeyhtiö Otava, 1940). A brief introductory study of the Finnish military elite is Antero Krekola, "Sotilaseliitti Suomessa," *Politiikka* 10 (1968): 18-25, 28. The most important challenge to the assumptions of both generations of Finnish officers is found in the novels of Väinö Linna: *The Unknown Soldier* (New York: G. P. Putnam's Sons, 1957) and the trilogy *Täällä Pohjantähden alla* (Porvoo: Werner Söderström Osakeyhtiö, 1959, 1960, and 1962). The inadequate and anonymous English translation of *The Unknown Soldier* is, perhaps mercifully, out of print, and the trilogy has not been published in English translation. For a summary of Linna's argument see Marvin Rintala, "Väinö Linna and the Finnish Condition," *Journal of Baltic Studies* 8 (Fall 1977): 223-31.

Index

94   Index

Gerich, Paul von, 68
Goebbels, Joseph, 42
Goering, Hermann, 42
Gurney, Ivor, 40

Hägglund, Woldemar, 83 n.76
Haig, Douglas, 36
Hanell, Edvard, 83 n.76
Heberle, Rudolf, 86
Heinrichs, Erik, 73, 76, 83 n.76
Heiskanen, Juho, 83 n.76
Hess, Rudolf, 42
Himmler, Heinrich, 42, 63 n.158
Hitler, Adolf, 12, 35, 41-44,
   61 n.133, 90
Hoover, Herbert, 12

Jägers, Finnish, 68-70, 73-76, 78 n.7,
   n.10, 79 n.13, 83 n.76, 92
Jünger, Ernst, 89

Kuropatkin, A. N., 72

Laatikainen, Taavetti, 83 n.76
Langemarck, battle of, 36
Ley, Robert, 42
Liddell Hart, Basil, 57 n.69, 67, 90
Literary generation. See Generation,
   literary
Lloyd George, David, 40, 46,
   60 n.119
Löfström, Ernst, 68, 70, 73-74
Lundqvist, Jarl, 83 n.76

Macmillan, Harold, 37, 62 n.152
Malmberg, Lauri, 76, 83 n.76
Mannerheim, Gustaf, 70-76, 77-
   78 n.3, 79 n.20, n.21, 81 n.42,
   n.48, n.50, 91-92
Mannheim, Karl, ix, 9, 15, 24 n.51,
   25 n.67, 48, 85-87

Marías, Julián, 21 n.28, 86
Marx, Karl, 11
Middlebrook, Martin, 90
Mill, James, 7
Mill, John Stuart, 7, 20 n.20
Mosley, Oswald, 32, 51 n.7
My Generation (Will Paynter), 5
My Generation of Politics and
   Politicians (W. T. R. Preston), 5

Nenonen, Vilho, 76, 83 n.79
Neumann, Sigmund, x, 86
Nicholas II, 35, 71-72

Oesch, Karl Lennart, 83 n.76
Öhquist, Harald, 83 n.76
Ortega y Gasset, José, 25 n.67,
   86-87
Österman, Hugo, 83 n.76
Owen, Wilfred, 33-35, 46-47, 89

Paasikivi, J. K., 17
Passchendaele, battle of, 36
Political generation. See Generation,
   political

Read, Herbert, 61 n.128, 90
Relander, Lauri Kristian, 75-76
Remarque, Erich Maria, 35-36, 89
Ribbentrop, Joachim von, 42
Richthofen, Manfred von, 34
Roosevelt, Franklin, 13
Rosenberg, Alfred, 42
Rosenberg, Isaac, 46
Ruhleben, 52 n.10
Russian Imperial Army officers,
   former, in Finnish Army, 68, 70-
   76, 83 n.79, 90-92. See also
   Mannerheim, Gustaf

About the Author

MARVIN RINTALA, Professor of Political Science at Boston College, Chestnut Hill, Massachusetts, is the author of *Four Finns: Political Profiles, Three Generations: The Extreme Right Wing in Finnish Politics* and of the article on political generations in the *International Encyclopedia of the Social Sciences.*